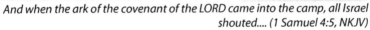

TABLE OF CONTENTS

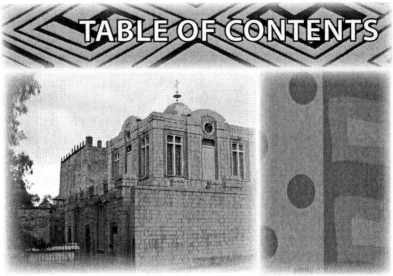

And when the ark of the covenant of the LORD came into the camp, all Israel shouted.... (1 Samuel 4:5, NKJV)

The
African American
Waking Up to God's
Missionary Call
Church

The
African American
Church

Waking Up to God's
Missionary Call

LEONIDAS A. JOHNSON

William Carey Library
Pasadena, California
www.WCLBooks.com

The African American Church:
Waking Up to God's Missionary Call

FIRST EDITION

Cover design: Melissa Dorr
Chief editor: Ken Graff
Layout/design: Olivia M. Cloud
Photographs: Leonidas A. Johnson (unless otherwise noted)

Published by William Carey Library
1605 E. Elizabeth Street, Pasadena, California 91104
www.WCLBooks.com

William Carey Library is a ministry of the U.S. Center for World Mission, Pasadena, California.

Printed in the United States of America

Library of Congress Cataloguing-in-Publication Data

Johnson, Leonidas A., 1959-
The African American Church: Waking Up to God's Missionary Call /
Leonidas A. Johnson.
    p.   cm.
Includes bibliographical references.
ISBN 0-87808-348-0 (alk. paper)
1. African Americans--Missions. I. Title.
BV2783.J64 2006
266.0089'96073--dc22
    2005033551

ACKNOWLEDGEMENTS

Thanks be to God, who gives us the victory through our Lord Jesus Christ.
(1 Corinthians 15:57)

SPECIAL THANKS TO...

Leon and Dolores Johnson, Alexander L. Johnson, Ivor and Porcya Duberry, Esker J. Harris, Barbara Rose, Olivia M. Cloud, Yalemzewd Worku, Cynthia Wierschen, Gail Oliver, Daniel Gebreselassie, Lemi Daba, Ralph Winter, Sharon Edwards, Suzanne Harlan, Jean Sorokin, Robert Stevens, Patrick Johnstone, Ken Graff, Paul E. Hawley and the many African American and Ethiopian heroes and soldiers of the cross who fought and fight the good fight of faith to the very end.

To God be the glory!

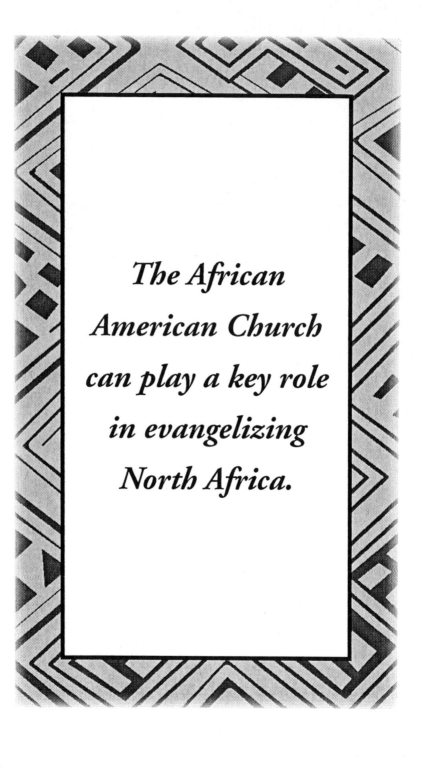

The African American Church can play a key role in evangelizing North Africa.

FOREWORD

Then they cried out to the LORD in their trouble.... (Psalm 107:6, NKJV)

GOD'S MISSIONARY CALL IS TO THE WHOLE CHURCH of Jesus Christ. This body of believers is a multi-ethnic and multi-lingual group of people from all around the world. This most certainly includes the African American Church. It reflects the future worshippers around the throne of God (Revelation 7:9-10). In 1992, my wife and I visited the U. S. Center for World Mission (USCWM) in Pasadena, California. We shared with the leadership that God had spoken to our hearts about reaching the world's unreached people groups who have never heard the Gospel of Jesus Christ. They were excited because God had also spoken to their hearts about mobilizing the African American church to help to evangelize these thousands of people of color.

This was the first time we ever heard of this vision. We did not know anything about the historical involvement of African Americans in missions. We had no idea of how many African American missionaries were on the field. We became aware that there was no documented information about African American missionaries at USCWM.

Getting this information would be a priority for us, if we were to accept the challenge to join the staff of missionaries at USCWM. These missionaries had to raise their financial support. Although we had never done this before, we accepted the challenge to join the missionary staff and live on campus. However, we were unable to raise our support in a timely manner. We were very discouraged because the African American pastors and churches with whom we shared the vision were not interested in supporting us as missionaries.

For the next seven years, as we pursued other interests, the vision of mobilizing the African American church to cross-cultural missions never left us. The Holy Spirit pursued us. During the fall of 1999, we met with Marylin Lewis—an African American missionary whom the Lord had raised up to mobilize the African American church. He had also sent her to USCWM. In His providence, He brought us together to develop the African American Center for World Mission. Not long after we met, Marylin went home to be with the Lord (February 2000). In November of this same year, my wife and I opened the office of the African American Mobilization Division of USCWM (now, the African American Center for World Mission, Inc.)

One month following Marylin's home-going, USCWM dedicated their prestigious *Mission Frontiers* April 2000 edition to the African American and Missions. Marylin Lewis was the guest editor of this issue. She wrote many of the articles that addressed the past and present of African American involvement in missions. This issue shook up the African American church.

Rev. Dr. Leonidas A. Johnson is one of the many African American leaders who were greatly influenced by this work. During 2001, I shared with him the vision of mobilizing the African American church to cross-cultural missions. I also challenged him to help fill the void of books related to African American missions. He caught and accepted the vision. Since then, he has made several short term missions trips to Africa (Ethiopia and Kenya). He has co-directed our missions education task force, which has produced the "Beyond Community Seminar Study Guide." He has now authored this masterful work, *The African American Church: Waking Up to God's Missionary Call.*

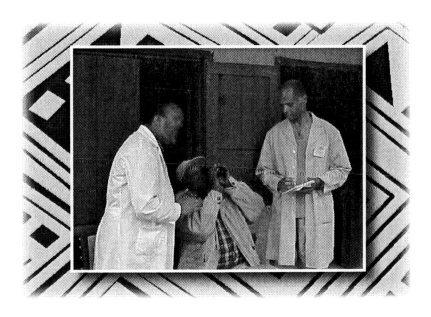

In this book, Dr. Johnson lucidly presents a strong case for the African American church as a key player in this new millennium of Christian missions. He points out that a large segment of the unreached peoples in the 10/40 Window is in North Africa and Arabia. These are people of color. The African American church can play a key role in evangelizing North Africa. He explores the strategic possibility of the African American Church partnering with Ethiopian missionaries to reach Arabia with the Gospel of Jesus Christ. These are some of the most resistant areas to the gospel message.

Just think: if the Gospel of the Kingdom can penetrate these areas in our lifetime, we will see the fulfillment of Matthew 24:14. This is a must-read book for anyone who believes John 3:16, "For God so loved the world…" and who loves the Lord Jesus and desires to see His vision of a redeemed humanity fulfilled (John 10:16; 4:23, Revelation 11:15)!

Rev. Ivor Duberry
General Director
African American Center for World Mission

Major Affinity Blocs and the 10/40 Window

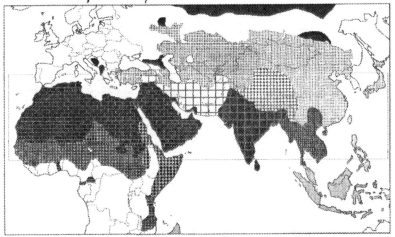

The least evangelized peoples of the world grouped for strategic purposes by linguistic, cultural, economic or political commonalities into eleven Affinity Blocs.

Arab (280 peoples)	**Horn of Africa** (40 peoples)	**Sub-Saharan** (400 peoples)	**Turkic** (260 peoples)	**Indo-Iranian** (380 peoples)
Indo-Aryan (560 peoples)	**Thai/Dai** (130 peoples)	**Tibetan** (80 peoples)	**Sinitic** (460 peoples)	**Malay** (580 peoples) **Eurasian** (1190 peoples)

Design: WEC Research Issue, 331 Sources: Patrick Johnstone, AD2000 and Beyond Movement, 1283

Therefore, any mission ministry within the church should not only reflect alignment with God's mission but also God's priority with respect to his mission.

CHAPTER ONE

God Is on Mission

Go therefore and make disciples of all nations, baptizing them in the name of the Father and of the Son and of the Holy Spirit. (Matthew 28:19, NKJV)

God loves you. In fact, God loves all the people he created to inhabit the earth. He gave us a free will so that we could choose, of our own free will, to love him. Adam and Eve's decision to disobey God's command is proof to all heaven and earth that human beings do indeed have free will (cf. Genesis 3:1-6). Even in the face of human defiance and disobedience, our heavenly Father continues to seek relationship with us. God desires that we freely choose to respond to his love with love and obedience. God honors us when we believe him and obey him. The Rev. Dr. Lynn Marcell reminds us that God's call to Adam, after he hid from the presence of God, demonstrates God's heart to pursue relationship with humanity, the crown of his creation (cf. Gen. 3:8-9).[1]

Our God is a missionary God. He always has been. God's mission to save humanity did not start in the New Testament with Jesus Christ. Ever since God formed Adam from the dust of the ground and breathed the breath of life into his nostrils, God has been on mission to save humanity from sin and death. Because of this thing called free will, God has been on mission to save us from ourselves ever since he created us! But how would God choose to fulfill his mission to fix the broken fellowship, to restore the sweet communion, to bridge the gap caused by sin--the consequences of free will? Jesus is the answer. Jesus suffered, bled and died on Mount Calvary, with love and obedience to God our Father, to fulfill God's mission.

The death, burial and resurrection of Christ Jesus constitute the foundation upon which our Lord and Savior established the church. Throughout the ages the church has had a positive effect on society. African American churches have traditionally participated in socioeconomic and humanitarian activities that demonstrate the love of God in practical ways through home and foreign mission programs. The Rev. Esker Jerome Harris of the National Baptist Convention, U.S.A., Inc., emphasizes that mission is not a part of the church--the church is part of God's mission.[2] God's mission existed before the church, and it is essential that church members understand that missions is not a secondary activity or program of the church. Rather, the church exists as an instrument of God's mission to redeem humanity back to himself. Therefore, any mission ministry within the church should reflect not only alignment with God's mission, but also God's priority with respect to his mission.

God's mission can be better be understood if viewed from four different viewpoints:

◆ biblical
◆ historical
◆ cultural
◆ strategic

My decision to talk about God's mission and the African American Church from these four perspectives is a strategy to build on a solid foundation of scientific research and other resources. A succinct presentation of these materials is available from the African American Center for World Mission in a one-day workshop entitled, "The African American and Missions: A Call Beyond Community." Also, the US Center for World Mission sponsors a "Perspectives" class that local churches may host. More resources are listed in chapter six and the appendix.

BIBLICAL

Is there biblical evidence that God has been on mission to save humanity from the very beginning? Absolutely! Despite our rebellion, God faithfully pursues us with loving dedication and commitment. Beginning with Genesis and ending with Revelation, book after book and scripture after scripture yields abundant evidence that God loves us and offers us hope that springs forth as an antidote to the poison called sin. In fact, in one way or another, every book of the Bible renders testimony of God's heart for the peoples of the world.

You may be familiar with the "red yellow-brick road," a road in the Bible that starts in the Garden of Eden.[3] The crimson red road of God's salvation leads to Calvary's Hill, where Jesus, the Lamb of God, shed His blood for the remission of our sins.[4]

However, you may not be as familiar with the "golden thread" in the Bible that runs from Genesis to Revelation.[5] This thread of scripture references demonstrates God's heart for all peoples of the earth and God's mission to save humanity from sin and death.

This may be shocking news to some, but God's mission to save humanity did not begin in the New Testament. God's mission did not start when Jesus gave the Great Commission (Matthew 28:19-20). The golden thread starts in Genesis, but not at the familiar Abrahamic Covenant of Genesis 12:1-3. Let us begin at the beginning!

The golden thread references prove that God had a missionary plan from the beginning. They start in the first book of the Old Testament at Genesis 3:14-15, continue into the New Testament, and conclude in the last chapter of the last book of the Bible at Revelation 22:17.

God has always been concerned about all people of the earth. God loves the people groups in Africa, Asia, Indonesia, Australia, South America, Central America, the Caribbean, the South Pacific, Canada, North America, Europe--wherever people live. No group has been forgotten or overlooked. Many people groups are still in spiritual bondage, waiting to hear human instruments, or gospelizers, echo the good news of great joy and proclaim the gospel message to their culture.

Gospelizers are God-sent messengers who bring through holistic witness the good news of Christ's presence and redeeming mission.[6] The Reverend Dr. Walter McCray thinks that the term should become well known in Christian vocabulary as a descriptive name for followers of Christ who bear witness on a mission. Seeking to popularize its use, Dr. McCray explains:

The passion of gospelizers is to spread Christ's presence with blessings of his salvation for all the lost, the least/poor, and the unwell in the harvest-fields of the world. Gospelizers bear a holistic witness for Christ by proclaiming good words, performing gracious works, and imparting great/miraculous workings of God. Working with Christ and his Church, the mission of gospelizers is to urgently and effectually reach out to people who apparently are yet unaffected by the Gospel's grace, truth, and power. Through their holistic witness of Christ's redeeming mission, the aims of gospelizers are to convert the lost, church the converted, and multiply the churches. Throughout each new generation, Christ has mandated gospelizers to fulfill their mission by gospelizing to every person, among all nations, to the uttermost parts of the earth, before the end of time, and until the Lord returns.[7]

In the Old Testament, God initiated a special relationship with a man of faith, Abraham, and used him to establish the nation of Israel. God then used Israel as an instrument to proclaim his name throughout the earth, to communicate to the peoples and nations of the earth, and to further his missionary plan to redeem people of all nations of the earth (see Genesis 12:1-3; Exodus 19:4-6; and Psalm 67).[8]

In the New Testament, God uses the Church--as he used the nation of Israel in the Old Testament--to further his missionary plan. African Americans can be viewed as a unique instrument within the church equipped with a special ability and role to play in God's overall missionary plan.

Following are some Old Testament references related to God's missionary plan to make himself known in all the earth and redeem human beings out of every tribe and tongue and people and nation (cf. Revelation 5:9).

Genesis 3:14-15; 12:1-3	Proverbs 18:10
Exodus 9:16; 19:4-6	Ecclesiastes 12:13-14
Leviticus 19:34	Song 1:5-6
Numbers 14:21 (c.f. Ex. 32:11)	Isaiah 25:6; 45:22
Deuteronomy 7:6-8	Jeremiah 1:5; 33:9
Joshua 4:23-24	Lamentations 3:22-23
Judges 2:11-13, 20-23	Ezekiel 36:23; 38:23
Ruth 1:16	Daniel 4:1-3; 7:13-14
1 Samuel 17:46	Hosea 2:23
2 Samuel 22:50	Joel 3:1-2, 12
1 Kings 8:41-43; 59-60	Amos 9:7, 10
2 Kings 19:19	Obadiah 1:15
1 Chronicles 16:23-24	Jonah 1:2; 3:1-10
2 Chronicles 6:32-33; 7:14	Micah 4:2-3; 5:4
Ezra 1:1-4	Nahum 1:5-7
Nehemiah 4:6-9	Habakkuk 3:12-13
Esther 8:7-8	Zephaniah 3:9-10
Job 1:6-8	Haggai 2:7
Psalms 33:18-19; 67:1-7;	Zechariah 2:11; 8:22
102:15-22; 107:1-3	Malachi 1:11

These scripture passages reveal a wonderful picture of a loving God on mission to redeem the people he created back to himself, while respecting free will. Since creation, God has stood—and continues to stand—with open arms, ready to embrace whoever chooses to respond to his call for relationship. He will continue to stand and welcome whosoever will come until he has representatives from every nation, tribe, people and tongue (Revelation 7:9-10).

HISTORICAL

What evidence, if any, is there in history that proves God is on mission and that he is making progress? It may be difficult to see the growing momentum and accelerating pace of God's mission movement through history with the wrong spectacles and/or when viewed from the wrong perspective. If we look at human history from a spiritual perspective, through the glasses of biblical revelation of God's missionary plan, then it is easy to see historical evidence that not only is God on mission but also that we are on the verge of completing his mission.

The US Center for World Mission gathers information that follows the progress of discipling the peoples of the world with respect to the Great Commission (Matthew 28:18-20). Information in their Perspectives program includes the work of Patrick Johnstone, director of research at WEC International and author of *Operation World*. Johnstone has tracked the progress of the preaching of the Gospel over its 2,000-year history. He has an illustration that shows that the number of peoples reached has dramatically increased within the past 100 years. He concludes by saying,

> Although many peoples are still unreached, the number is only a fraction of that of 100 years ago. The goal is attainable in our generation—if we mobilize prayer and effort and work together to disciple the remaining least reached peoples.[9]

God is not losing a tug-of-war-like battle with evil. God has been carefully moving his mission plan forward through history. From one perspective, there has been a growing tide of evil around the world. From another perspective, there has been continuous growth in the spread of Christianity around the

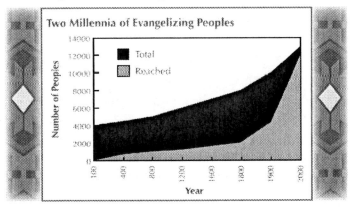

world. In fact, current research tells us that recent growth of Christianity around the world has been explosive.[10] From either perspective, the acceleration of evil in the world or the recent acceleration of the spread of the Gospel around the world, one may conservatively conclude that the long-awaited return of Jesus Christ is near. We are in the midst of end-time ministry!

Dr. Ralph Winter, founder of the US Center for World Mission, has divided human history into ten 400-year periods as a teaching device to help us follow the unfolding drama of God's missionary plan. Let us briefly review human history from a spiritual perspective to get a big picture of God's movement in history. Then we will move into a discussion on God's mission and African American history.

In viewing Dr. Winter's ten epochs of redemptive history, it would be helpful to note four different mission mechanisms God has used to spread his message and advance his mission, with or without the full cooperation of his chosen nation. Generally speaking, the mechanisms are: *voluntary go; involuntary go; voluntary come;* and *involuntary come*.[11]

Voluntary go (outreach) is when, out of obedience, the people of God obey God's command and go throughout the world to share God's missionary plan of salvation (e.g., Abraham to Canaan, Paul to the Gentiles, George Liele to Jamaica, and the Rev. Daniel Coker to Sierra Leone, Africa). *Involuntary go* (outreach) is when God accomplishes his missionary plan and blesses the nations even when his people do not voluntarily go (e.g., Joseph involuntarily went to Egypt). Jesus said, "And I, if I am lifted up from the earth, will draw all peoples to Myself" (John 12:32).

Voluntary come (draw) is when people voluntarily come to where blessing-relationship with God exists (e.g., the Queen of Sheba voluntarily came to King Solomon). *Involuntary come* (draw) is when people involuntarily come to where blessing-relationship with God exists (e.g., African slaves involuntarily came to America).

With respect to African slaves involuntarily coming to America many Americans believe that enslaved Africans were uncivilized and had no knowledge of Christianity prior to arriving in America. Please note that the Ethiopian Church reports that Christianity first reached Ethiopia in the first century at the time of the apostles. Further, most historians agree that it was declared the official state religion in the fourth century by King Ezana, making Ethiopia one of the oldest Christian civilizations in the world, if not the oldest.[12] Also note that many African slaves may have already been exposed to and worshiped the God who delivered the Israelites out of Egypt. In fact, Lamin Sanneh, Professor of Missions and World Christianity at Yale Divinity School, has done research that indicates Christianity reached the west coast of Africa as early as 1402.[13]

It is important to incorporate two epochs of God's redemptive history not in Dr. Winter's analysis. An African American perspective of God's missionary plan is not complete, I believe, without considering the Prediluvian Period and the Period of Hamitic Rule. But let us first review Dr. Winter's list of ten epochs.

Ten Epochs of Redemptive History:
The First Half 2000-1 B.C.

Dr. Winter begins the story of God's redemptive plan with the calling of Abraham in Genesis 12. According to Dr. Winter:

> The first eleven chapters of Genesis constitute a scary "introduction" to the entire problem, indeed, to the plot of the entire Bible. Those few pages describe three things:

> 1) a glorious and "good" original creation; 2) the entrance of a rebellious and destructive evil—[a] superhuman, demonic person resulting in: 3) a humanity caught up in that rebellion and brought under the power of that evil person....From Genesis 12 to the end of the Bible, and indeed until the end of time, there unfolds the single, coherent drama of "the Kingdom strikes back."[14]

The first half of Winter's redemptive history is, then:

Period I (2000 B.C. — 1600 B.C.) — Patriarchs
Period II (1600 B.C. — 1200 B.C.) — Captivity
Period III (1200 B.C. — 800 B.C.) — Judges
Period IV (800 B.C. — 400 B.C.) — Kings
Period V (400 B.C. — 1 B.C.) — Post-Exile[15]

Ten Epochs of Redemptive History: The Second Half A.D. 1-2000[16]

Period I —Winning the Romans (A.D. 1-400)

The gospel advanced by all four mission mechanisms. The gospel flowed along trade routes as well as throughout the social strata. During early centuries, Christianity was the one religion with no nationalistic political identity. As such, it appealed to many throughout the empire—and beyond. Once it became the official imperial religion, Christianity began to carry the political and cultural stigma of being Roman. This slowed down the advance which was already under way in areas beyond the Roman Empire, particularly where Rome was despised or feared. Winter suggests a new way to look at what might be regarded as heresy. There were different flavors of Christian faith that differed slightly in the details but gave people a way to espouse their own brand of Christianity. Thus, areas hostile to the Roman Empire were more likely to embrace what the Roman Empire/ church considered heresy, such as Arianism.

Period II —Winning the Barbarians (A.D. 400-800)

The barbarian tribes invaded the Roman Empire and became more thoroughly evangelized. This period was an expression of the voluntary-come mechanism. European monastic orders were also established during the later part of this time. Some orders became expressly missionary and followed a voluntary-go pattern. Barbarian tribes, such as the Goths, Visigoths, Vandals, and Anglo-Saxons, invaded most of western and central Europe. Though Rome lost half its empire, the barbarian world gained the Christian faith in the process.

Period III —Winning the Vikings (A.D. 800-1200)

The Viking conquerors were themselves conquered by the faith of their captives. This demonstrates a voluntary-come mechanism. The gospel spread to Scandinavia and other northern European areas. "Usually monks sold as slaves or Christian girls forced to be witnesses ... eventually won these strangers in the north."[17]

Period IV—Winning the Saracens (Muslims)? (A.D. 1200-1600)

Once northern Europeans capitulated to "the counterattack of the Gospel," they became leaders in the greatest perversion of mission in history:

the crusades. Using a deeply flawed voluntary-go pattern, they destroyed and conquered territory without any success in extending the blessing of the gospel to the Muslims, sometimes referred to as the Saracens. The crusades were an abortion of advance. Tragically, the crusades warped mission into conquest. The effect of the crusades reverberates to this day in most of the Muslim world. The beginnings of colonial expansion brought some advance of Christian faith, but not of Protestant faith.

Period V —To the Ends of the Earth (A.D. 1600-2000)

The Catholic expansion continued and then was suddenly wounded around 1800 with Napoleon's ransacking of Europe and the growing popularity of atheism, deism, and humanism. At the same time the voluntary-go mechanism of the Protestant mission movement finally took off. Protestant missionaries reached across the globe. The Protestant movement first advanced to the coastlands with or without colonial expansion. Then came another wave to the inland areas. Finally, the focus shifted to reaching all the peoples of the earth.

The Missing Links:
Twelve Epochs of God's Redemptive History?

The two epochs of God's redemptive history missing from Dr. Winter's masterful work occur prior to the call of Abraham and link God's call to Abraham with God's call to Adam.

The first epoch is *the Prediluvian Period*. It covers the time from the Fall in the Garden of Eden to the Flood (?—4000 B.C.). This first period starts with God's call to Adam in the Garden. When Adam and Eve disobeyed God and ate the forbidden fruit, fellowship with God was broken. Adam, instead of running to God, ran from God and hid from the presence of God (Genesis 3:8-10). It was God who initiated steps to fix the problem and restore the broken fellowship. God showed Adam how to become reconciled back to God (Genesis 3:21), and Adam in turn was responsible for teaching this to Cain, Abel (Genesis 4:3-5), and the rest of his family (voluntary-come mechanism).

Arguably, the best source of extra-biblical information about the antediluvian (prediluvian) period and ancient times is Africa, the origin of humanity. Genetic data from dozens of researchers in the field of population genetics point to a common African human origin. This has led genetic genealogists to universally support the "Out of Africa" theory.[18] Research in paleoanthropology has given rise to the belief that the Ethiopian section of the African Rift Valley was the original home of humanity.[19] Many of the contributions Ethiopia has to offer modern civilization are buried in ancient archives of the Ethiopian Orthodox Tewahedo Church (EOTC). Kessis Kefyalew Merahi, an ordained priest who has held several EOTC leadership positions, writes that the church's oral and written tradition affirms the following:

> In 1000 B.C. (4500 B.C.) a man named Ori (Aram) is known to have come to Ethiopia and to have built his town in a place called Merwie (Meroe) in Nubia. The person was the first in a dynasty of 21 successive kings whose combined

reign lasted for 1256 years. This dynasty was known as the Tribe of Orit.

That period was followed by the Great Deluge which destroyed the world. Five hundred-thirty-one years after the Great Flood, in 2787 B.C. (2713), a person by the name of Kam [Ham] (Kussa) came to Ethiopia and settled in the same Merwie (Meroe) in Nubia, beginning a dynasty to be made up of 22 successive kings. The total duration of their reign was 728 years, and the period is known as the Era of Kam (Kussa).

In 3515 B.C. (1985) the tribes of Sem [Shem] (Yoktan) came to Ethiopia when the people of India's King Rama were inhabiting the country. The newcomers fought against Rama's people, expelling them from Ethiopia. Fifty-two successive kings, who ruled Ethiopia for a total of 1003 years, belonged to the Sem tribe.

In 4518 B.C. (982) Menelik I returned to Ethiopia, along with the Ark of the Covenant (Tabote Tsion), and accompanied by 12,000 people from the 12 tribes of Israel. He put the Ark in Axum and became the progenitor of 67 successive kings. The aggregate duration of their reign was 982 years until 5,500 B.C....

The last of Ethiopia's reigning monarchs was His Majesty Emperor Haile Sellassie I, who was crowned on November 2, 1930, and ruled the country for forty-four years. A total of 331 kings are known to have ruled Ethiopia.... Ethiopia is extremely rich in history. "The problem of many African Countries is lack

of historical context, whereas the problem of
Ethiopia is the plentiful of its history (Professor
Richard Pankhurst)."[1]

Certainly the time is come for Ethiopian history to be fully
studied. The world drips with anticipation for such a time as
this. It is time for buried historical sites to be dug out, tombs and
tunnels to be explored, and historical materials and documents
to be collected and examined. As this is carefully done, I believe
marvelous wonders and attractions will be brought to light
that have been guarded for centuries and held in safe accord
by heroic Ethiopian soldiers of the faith and the Ethiopian
Orthodox Tewahedo Church. Indeed, Ethiopia shines as a
gleaming example of good stewardship of God's treasures.

The second epoch is *the Period of Hamitic Rule*. It roughly
covers the period from the Flood to the call of Abraham (4000
B.C.—2000 B.C.). Noah's three sons repopulated the earth after
the deluge (see Genesis 9:19). From Ham came the Hamites
(or Hamitic people), from Shem came the Semites (or the
Semitic people), and from Japheth came Japhethites (or the
Japhetic people). According to William Dwight McKissic, Sr.,
"The name Ham means 'dark or black,' Shem means 'dusky or
olive-colored,' and Japheth means 'bright or fair.'"[21]

McKissic divides history into three ages. Generally speaking,
he writes, each race has been given 2000 years to reign: the
Reign of Ham — 4000 B.C. to 2000 B.C.; the Reign of Shem
— 2000 B.C. to 300 B.C.; the Reign of Japheth — 300 B.C.
to the present.[22] Most scholars agree that Ham was the father
of indigenous African peoples.[23] Ham's descendents politically
and culturally dominated the early world. McKissic writes,

> The sons of Ham ruled Shinar (Sumer) as early as 4000
> B.C. Hamites ruled Ethiopia from 3500 B.C. to this present

> day. Hamites ruled Egypt from 3500 B.C. to the Persian conquest of Egypt in 525 B.C. Hamites ruled Canaan from 4000 B.C. to 1200 B.C. and Mesopotamia from 4000 B.C. to 2350 B.C.....Hamites people ruled India from 3000 B.C. until conquest of the Persians in 500 B.C. In every instance, these people led extremely advanced civilizations and culture.[24]

One of Ham's great descendents was Nimrod, perhaps the greatest leader the world has known. Nimrod was a liberator, a king, a kingdom builder, a creative pioneer, and a spiritual, progressive leader, and there is not one hint that Nimrod was violent or oppressed other peoples.[25] He built great cities like Babel. When Nimrod decided to build the Tower of Babel, scripture reveals that his motives for building the tower were noble: (1) religious—so that the top might reach heaven; (2) pride—"and let us make a name"; and (3) unity—lest they be scattered.

Scripture also reveals that this one decision was made independent of God, and God did not approve. Nimrod's (voluntary-come mechanism) approach to God was wrong. Nimrod's superior leadership skill and abilities disturbed God (Genesis 11:6-7; cf. 10:8-11). God did not want all the people to continue in error because of the error of one great and mighty leader. I believe this concern triggered God to move to the next phase of his missionary strategy for reaching humanity.

Instead of reaching out to all the people of the earth as a single collective group through one leader (e.g., Nimrod), he would divide the people of the earth into many different people groups and reach groups of people through these smaller people groups. And later, from one chosen people group (Israelites/Hebrews/Jews) would come the Messiah, a personal Savior through which God could reach individuals from each people group personally. I believe God's decision to divide the people of the earth into different, smaller people groups at Babel was a strategy to more effectively reach the growing masses of morally independent people of the earth, not a judgment for the people's desire to build the Tower of Babel (Genesis 11:3-4, 6-9).

The 12 Epochs of God's Redemptive History (Winter and Johnson)

God's mission to reconcile the broken relationship with humanity has a long history, indeed. The 12 epochs of God's Redemptive History (Winter and Johnson) are:

Period I (?–4000 B.C.) .... Prediluvian
Period II (4000–2000 B.C.) .... Hamitic Rule
Period III (2000–1600 B.C.) .... Patriarchs
Period IV (1600–1200 B.C.) .... Captivity
Period V (1200–800 B.C.) .... Judges
Period VI (800–400 B.C.) .... Kings
Period VII (400–1 B.C.) .... Post-Exile
Period VIII (A.D. 1–400) .... Winning the Romans
Period IX (A.D. 400–800) .... Winning the Barbarians
Period X (A.D. 800–1200) .... Winning the Vikings
Period XI (A.D. 1200–1600) .... Winning the Saracens/Muslims?
Period XII (A.D. 1600–2000) .... To the Ends of the Earth

Again, the Hamitic Period has great significance with respect to discussion of the African American Church and God's missionary call. We learn that African Americans are the descendants of Ham and of the founders of modern civilization. We also learn from this period the key to recognizing the implicit presence of blacks in the Bible (descendants of Ham in the Table of Nations, Genesis 10:6-20). We learn the argument that circulates in some black communities that the Bible is a white man's book, written by the white man, for the white man, is not biblically sound. We also learn the argument that circulates in other African American communities that color does not matter is not biblically sound.

The full counsel of the word of God teaches us that there is a large black presence in the Bible and that black people are important to God. Let us teach truth without distortion as faithful stewards of the mysteries of God (1 Corinthians 4:1). Most important, as we move into end-time ministry, as we reflect on our biblical heritage, let us not contend with our Semitic and Japhetic brothers and sisters but join together, seeing we all have had opportunity to lead the world, each with faults, and jointly make peace with God in the manner he has instructed us and embrace God's missionary plan to reach the lost at all cost.

GOD'S MISSION AND THE AFRICAN AMERICAN

Now let us review God's mission and the African American. I have been to Africa several times, and a common question from is "Where are the African Americans?" To help understand how to intelligently handle this important question, we are reprinting (by permission) a pivotal article by missionary Marylin Lewis from a special edition of *Mission Frontiers* magazine. Lewis, working with the Rev. Ivor and Porcha Duberry, inspired the development of the African American Mobilization Division at the US Center for World Mission, which later evolved into the African American Center for World Mission, founded by Rev. Duberry.

"Overcoming Obstacles: The Broad Sweep of the African American and Missions"

Since the later 18th century, African Americans have displayed an interest in world evangelization. Some scholars have argued that this interest was due to escapism—a desire to leave the racist and hostile environment of America. Others have argued more positively that their involvement was motivated by a simple obedience to the Great Commission. While both factors were at work, obedience best explains the activity from the 1770s to the present day.

Why, for example, did Prince Williams leave the shores of America, travel to Nassau and establish a church? Without any biographies or autobiographies, we cannot make a definitive statement about his motive. But the church planted as the fruit of his labor makes escapism seem suspect.

Several years later, former American slaves and ministers George Liele, David George, Hector Peters, and Sampson Calvert sailed from Nova Scotia where they had established the African Baptist Church and journeyed to Sierra Leone to plant a new church.

By the 1800s all of the major Protestant denominations in the United States had stations in Africa and utilized the African American as the missionary of choice. A number of reasons contributed to this, including the belief that the descendants of former Africans could better adapt to the environment and were less likely to die from disease. Additionally, the majority of white missionaries were then looking towards the continent of Asia as a mission field— not towards Africa. At least seventy African American missionaries represented these organizations, serving from 1790 to 1820.

After the establishment of the independent denominations AME and AMEZ, African American interest in world evangelization grew—and they began sending missionaries. These denominations represented the first real independence movements in the African American community. The conviction grew that they could and should send and sponsor their own missionaries. Being encouraged by the African American church, the intelligentsia and newspapers, the community agreed that it was the will of God for them to become involved in mission, "to return home" and help in the evangelization of Africa.

But why would someone recently freed from slavery desire to leave comfortable surroundings, family, friends and material possessions to travel around the world to convert people to Christ? Few secular scholars understood or adequately conveyed the pull of the Holy Spirit calling individuals to serve on the mission field. The writings of the early African American missionaries make it clear that the desire to fulfill the Great Commission was the motivating factor for missionary service—a God-given burden for the uttermost parts.

Africa became the major field of service for early African American missionaries. One obvious and very understandable reason was their affection for the land of their forefathers. But the continent was portrayed by the press, public, and people as being in grave need of workers. African Americans selected Africa and decided that God had called them to bring Christianity and culture. The early African American missionaries believed that if the Africans worshiped, obeyed, and submitted to the true God and accepted the best of Western culture, they would be able to control their own country, build their own nation and establish their own destiny.

Toward the close of the 19th century, white missionary presence in Africa began to rise. The writings of European discoverers emphasized the need of the African to receive salvation and a "civilizing lifestyle." Europeans were encouraged to come to Africa and serve in the missionary effort. The discovery of effective medical treatment and immunizations made the continent all the more appealing. Parallel to a growing interest in the spiritual state of Africans was the growth in commercial and colonial endeavors on the continent.

As Europeans entered Africa and established colonial governments, they questioned the utilization of the African American missionary. The common sentiment of colonial governments was that blacks from North America should not be allowed to enter into some areas—as they were unduly influenced by democracy and the Pan-African and back-to-Africa movements. The fear: that they would encourage Africans to rebel against colonial authority. All of these fears—justified and unjustified—increased tension between missionaries and the colonial governments. The sentiment of some that African Americans did not make good missionaries—that they were ineffective in spreading the Gospel—did not help matters. Also, deaths on the mission field disproved the belief that the African American has any better propensity for adaptation to the climate and fighting disease.

Hence, by the turn of the 20th century, very few African American missionaries were encouraged or sponsored by the white missionary groups. Rather, they were financed by African American churches who felt a special burden for the evangelization of Africa. By and large, black mission work was done in nations controlled by colonial governments. (An exception was Liberia—the only nation in West Africa not officially under colonial authority. Black missionaries there had a greater degree of liberty.) Even if unofficially, black missionaries could serve in areas undesirable for European settlers, such as east Africa.[26] In southern Africa, they could serve but were not accorded the same respect as white missionaries. By the 1920s, African Americans were generally discouraged from—and at times prohibited from—entering the African field.

Though few in number, the African American missionaries made strides in the propagation on the Gospel in the key places they served—west, central and southern Africa. Beyond the planting of churches, medical facilities and schools were established; social reform movements and Bible translation began as well as a growth in industrial and commercial enterprises. All the while, African Americans gained tremendous knowledge of traditional African life. And the example of the African American missionary certainly provided the African with the visible hope that self-government is a possibility.

The Golden Age of Missions

As every movement has it ups and downs, the period 1890-1910 may well be seen as a Golden Age. Some 200 African American missionaries were serving throughout the world—mostly throughout Africa, but also the West Indies. At this time the two large supporting blocks were the African-American church and white missions organizations.

This era witnessed the establishment of the Presbyterian Congo Mission station, a station that was manned by African Americans and led by African American William Sheppard. This is also the era of Emma B. Delaney, a National Baptist missionary who assisted in the establishment of mission stations and educational sites.[27] Another dynamic figure of this Golden Age was Bishop Henry Turner of the AME denomination who supported African missions and felt led of the Lord to encourage blacks to enter the mission arena, supporting the Motherland, Africa.

Hindrances

The period from 1920-1930 could be referred as the Hindrances Period—with a number of factors discouraging the entrance of African Americans into missionary work. Colonial governments that refused to accord equitable treatment to the African American missionaries provided the primary obstacle for mission service. Labeling them as "undesirable aliens," they felt that the rise of Pan Africanism, Marcus Garvey and questions of equal rights in America might unduly influence Africans. Missionaries such as Sheppard, Delaney and James East dealt with treatment that was clearly discriminatory and racist. In several publications, African Americans complained that no matter how trained they were, they could not find access to the missionary field of Africa.

In 1920, the Portuguese government changed its missionary regulations, insisting that all future missionaries serving in its colonies know Portuguese (as taught in Portugal) and be assigned by the colonial government. Another hindrance came from the refusal of white missionary organizations to utilize the African American in world evangelization, so as not to offend the colonial governments. Understandably, the black missionary felt unwelcome and unwanted in Africa. The American government complied with the colonial governments and refused to grant visas to certain areas.

By the mid 1930s the African American missionary was virtually absent from the field. Several missionaries were still serving—including Montrose Waite—but for the most part, African Americans understood that they were not welcome.

Redefinition

The period of Redefinition (1935–present) has occurred in the African American church itself. Maybe in part a response to racism and discrimination, the leadership of the church developed a "protective mechanism" for missionary participation. The church changed the definition of missionary. Missionaries were no longer those who journeyed to another country or culture to take out the Gospel. Now, a missionary was defined, essentially, as "a woman who did good works and who taught the Bible in small women-led groups." Missionary work included all of the things that women did in the church—visiting the sick, cleaning the church and feeding the homeless. However, none of those activities involved taking out the Gospel. All of these endeavors ought to be considered good works, but not missions proper—as spoken of in Matthew 28:18-20.

What happened in the African American church? The change in definition allowed it to demonstrate that it still had "missionaries"—though they were home-based. Cross-cultural, foreign missionaries vanished completely. Very few African Americans carried the Gospel into another land, even though there were hundreds of missionaries in every denomination. Missionaries were those who worked at home. White missionaries traveled, but African American missionaries worked in the community because "the needs are so great here."

In the early sixties, another redefinition occurred in the African American community: the formation of black-led missionary organizations outside of the church denominational groups. These new organizations restored the biblical perspective and ignited vision for missions. For the first time missionary organizations such as Carver International Mission, Have Christ Will Travel, and eventually Ambassador Fellowship were established to assist in the thrust of world evangelization. African Americans now have missionary organizations with dedicated missionaries and missiologists focusing upon the task of world evangelization.

The Great Age

Today, in the year 2000, we have seen the groundwork laid and are expecting another wide thrust of African American involvement in world evangelization. This period may be called the Great Age of Mission. My belief is that it will be larger and greater than any other involvement of the African American community. It will focus upon all areas of the world—not just Africa. Youth as well as adults will enter into missionary endeavors. This period will witness the increased involvement of short as well as long-term service.

African Americans are now looking seriously at the 10/40 Window, and they are planning how they can be involved. The possibilities are exhilarating.[28]

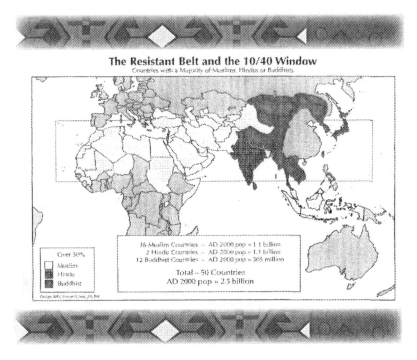

The Resistant Belt and the 10/40 Window
Countries with a Majority of Muslims, Hindus or Buddhists

Over 50%
Muslim
Hindu
Buddhist

36 Muslim Countries – AD 2000 pop = 1.1 billion
2 Hindu Countries – AD 2000 pop = 1.1 billion
12 Buddhist Countries – AD 2000 pop = 305 million

Total – 50 Countries
AD 2000 pop = 2.5 billion

(The 10/40 Window is the area between the latitudes 10° and 40° north of the equator and between the Atlantic and Pacific oceans. See below under "Strategy.")

The above article gives us a good understanding of early African American participation and reasons for lack of participation in God's mission to unreached people groups of the world. As you can see, participation in God's mission is not a new thing to African Americans. As David Cornelius writes, "From the time slaves began accepting Christianity, it was in their hearts to carry the Gospel of Christ not only back to their fatherlands, but also to other parts of the world."[29] In fact, the Bible tells us that it was the Hamites (Africans) who first serve as missionaries to the Japhethites (Europeans), and yet many African Americans are led to believe Europeans first served as missionaries to Africans. In fact some European Christians may imply (unintentionally) that African Americans have no interest or heritage in international missions because of the recent lack of observable presence of African Americans on the foreign mission field.

During the persecution that followed after Stephen was martyred in Jerusalem, it was the descendents of Ham, Africans, who first preached the Lord Jesus to the Europeans (Hellenists).

> Now those who were scattered after the persecution that arose over Stephen traveled as far as Phoenicia, Cyprus, and Antioch, preaching the word to no one but the Jews only. But some of them were men from Cyprus and Cyrene, who, when they had come to Antioch, spoke to the Hellenists, preaching the Lord Jesus. And the hand of the Lord was with them, and a great number believed and turned to the Lord. (Acts 11:19-21, NKJV)

These bold missionaries from Cyprus and Cyrene were black. The Bible does not explicitly say so, but we know they were black implicitly from study of scripture. With regard to Cyrene, we learn from Acts 2:7-11 that Cyrene was next to Libya: "...Egypt and the parts of Libya adjoining Cyrene..." (Acts 2:10). From the Table of Nations in Genesis 10 we learn that Put was a son of Ham. Put is also translated as Libya.

> Put is the third son/descendent of Ham, the only one with no descendents named in the Table.... By name Put is mentioned eight times in the Bible (Genesis 10:6, 1 Chronicles 1:8; Isaiah 66:19; Jeremiah 46:9; Ezekiel 27:10;

30:5; Nahum 3:9). According to Josephus, Put was the founder of Libya, whose inhabitants were called Putites. The Septuagint translates Put into "Libya." Libya is located in northern Africa west of Egypt. Other scholars identify Put with the Punt of Egyptian inscription in East African Somaliland.

Shishak (Sheshonq I, ca. 945-915 B.C.) was an Egyptian pharaoh of Libyan origin, and founder of the Twenty-second Dynasty (ca. 945-730). He is mentioned in 1 Kings 11:40; 14:25; 2 Chronicles 12:2ff. in relations with Jeroboam I (providing him refuge), and with Rehoboam (invading Palestine).[30]

Cyrene was located in northern Africa!

With regard to the mention of Cyprus, consider the following information gleaned by Dr. Walter McCray:

Two of the biblical inhabitants of Cyprus were Barnabas (Acts 4:36), and Bar-Jesus (Acts 13:6ff.). Could it be verified that either of the forementioned were Black?! Contact of Blacks with the island of Cyprus occurred at various historical points. It was conquered by Thutmose III of the 18th Dynasty (1501-1447 B.C.); it was influenced much by Crete; the Phoenicias made settlements on the island in the 9th and 8th c. B.C.; it was conquered by Aahmes (Amasis) of Egypt and held to 526 B.C.; it fell under the domain of the Ptolemies of Egypt (323 B.C.); and again under their domain in 294-258 B.C.

The most convincing explanation of Negroid stone figures found in Cyprus is that the sculptures were portraits of Ethiopians in the civil and military service of the Egyptians during Egyptian occupation of the island under Amasis [king of Egypt] (568-525 B.C.).

A striking piece of corroborative evidence for the presence of Ethiopians in Cyprus is the traditional opinion of the Cyprians themselves, recorded by Herodotus, that one component of their archaeological evidence, together with the fact that Egyptians had a long history of recruiting Ethiopians, tends to confirm the view that the figures depicted Negroes present during the military occupation of Cyprus in the sixth century. It is not possible to determine the size of the Negroid contingents among the Egyptian forces, but it does not seem likely that the Cyprians would have included Ethiopians in a statement of population statistics—the others mentioned being Salaminians, Athenians, Arcadians, Cythnians, and Phoenicians—had the numbers been negligible.[31]

There is a strong implicit presence of blacks in the Bible. Not only did these Hamites from Cyprus and Cyrene (Simeon called Niger, Lucius of Cyrene) serve as early missionaries to Europeans, they also took part in commissioning Paul to the mission field (Acts 13:1-3). Lucius of Cyrene, like Simeon of Cyrene (Mark 15:21) and Simeon called Niger would be considered explicit evidence of the presence of blacks in the Bible. African Americans indeed have a great heritage as faithful servants of the *missio Dei*, the Mission of God. Who can deny it?

The way the Gospel is presented can very easily get twisted because the culture of the presenter differs from the culture of the listener. African Americans are very sensitive to this issue. The way the Gospel has been presented to many blacks in America would make one think that the Bible is a book about white people for white people and that there is little if any black presence in the Bible. Likewise one might also think that African Americans have no interest in God's mission. African Americans are equipped by their history of racial discrimination in American to be excellent missionaries and faithful stewards of the wonderful mysteries of God.

More information about the history of African Americans and God's mission is available from the African American Center for World Mission. Especially recommended are *The African American Experience in World Mission: A Call Beyond Community.*[32] and Dr. Jim Sutherland's dissertation, "African American Underrepresentation in Intercultural Missions: Perceptions of Black Missionaries and the Theory of Survival/Security."[33]

CULTURAL

What cultural evidence is there that God is a missionary God? With the dispersion of the people at the Tower of Babel, God initiated a different strategy for reaching the peoples of the earth. Instead of attempting to reach people as a single culture and unit, God divided the people of the world into small groups by confounding their language. Today God's mission strategy is to reach each ethnic group or people group. Different ethnic or people groups have different ways of communicating, different value systems, different ways of perceiving and understanding the world. All these factors fall under the banner of culture. God works within different cultures to accomplish his missionary plan.

As you may suspect, social and cultural differences can greatly inhibit the progress of the Gospel. The Gospel readily spreads among different cultures where it has been established, but it may not easily jump from one subgroup to another within a people group because of cultural barriers (e.g., sociopolitical, economic, prejudicial) between peoples. Sometimes when people of different cultures hear the Gospel, they view certain practices as being hostile to their culture, making it impossible for them to follow Christ openly without abandoning their cultural identity and significant relationships.

Unfortunately, in the past most missionaries in Africa corrupted the ministry of spreading the Gospel with other private or national imperialistic agendas, such as spreading Eurocentric Western culture, government expansion via colonialism, and commercial/materialistic gain. Instead of empowering the communities they entered, they at times facilitated looting, robbing, and stripping these communities of their natural resources, national treasures, cultural dignity, and wealth (e.g., the 1868 British invasion of Meqdela to free British missionaries held 'hostage' and the shameful looting of Ethiopian national treasures by British forces and their entourage).[34]

To more easily understand the job God has called us to do in light of different cultures of the world, it is important to look at the task from the perspectives of the evangelist/missionary (E-scale) and from the point of the potential disciple (P-scale). E-scale stands for *Evangelistic* distance and represents the cultural distance between evangelists and potential hearers of the gospel.[35] P-scale stands for *People* distance and represents the cultural distance between potential converts and churches that may welcome them into fellowship.[36] For example, many African Americans are culturally closer to many African cultures than are Europeans. Because of cultural factors it may be more effective for an African American to share the Gospel with an African from an African American perspective than it is for a European to share the Gospel with an African from a European perspective.

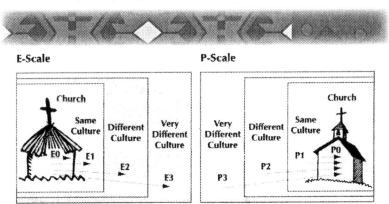

The **E-Scale** helps compare the cultural distances that Christians need to move in order to communicate the gospel with others. E0 refers to evangelism of church-going Christians. E1 extends to the very same culture through one barrier, that of "church culture." E2 evangelism presses into a close, but still different, culture. E3 evangelism pushes to very different cultures.

The **P-Scale** is more than a mirror of the E-Scale. The P-Scale helps compare the different cultural distances that potential converts need to move in order to join the nearest church.

STRATEGIC

What strategies exist that demonstrate that God is a missionary God? All creation reveals that God is a God of design and strategy. God created the universe and placed humans in it so that he might have fellowship and relationship with humans. In order for authentic relationship to exist, God created humans with a free will that human beings may freely choose to have relationship with God. In God's plan, those who do not choose to have relationship with God must deal with the consequence of eternal separation from God. With the tremendous power of moral freedom comes great responsibility. By design, God simplified the moral choices we need to make. We must choose to have life (by his grace through faith in Jesus Christ) or eternal death by default. God is a God of design, and as his children, made in his image, we should mimic our heavenly Father and do things with design and creativity.

When it comes to fulfilling God's mission to unreached people groups (i.e., a group within which no indigenous community of believing Christians is able to evangelize this people group[37]) it makes no sense to duplicate efforts and fumble over one another in trying to accomplish the task he has give us. Those mistakes have already been made in the past. Let us learn from past mission experiences and history. This means we must coordinate efforts and work together!

It cannot be emphasized too much: We must work together! The beauty of the African American Center for World Mission (AACWM) is that its establishment marks a strategy to work in partnership with the US Center for World Mission. It will serve as a nondenominational clearinghouse, a place where mission-related information and data such as what has been and is being done and by whom can be collected and disbursed. AACWM is in a good position to make recommendations for future efforts and strategies toward accomplishing the remaining task, offering tools for assessing the effectiveness of African American mission efforts, and coordinating African American mission efforts.

Because of a sovereign promise God made in his word we know there will be a church movement in every people group. Jesus said, "This gospel of the kingdom will be preached in all the world as a witness to all the nations, and then the end will come" (Matthew 24:14). Dr. Winter has written:

> If only enough of the world's great cloud of believers can be awakened to how little there is left to do! How can this be possible with over 6 billion people and less than 3/4 billion committed Christians? The answer is in the unique strategy of the Great Commission in Matthew 28. Jesus did not say "go and talk to every individual in the world." He said to multiply by making disciples within all *ethne* or peoples.[38]

Most unreached people groups live in North Africa and Asia where Islam, Hinduism, and Buddhism are the dominant religions. This region is sometimes referred to as the 10/40 Window. The 10/40 Window is the area between the latitudes 10° and 40° north of the equator and between the Atlantic and Pacific oceans. Basically, the countries in or near the 10/40 Window that are under-evangelized have only 35 percent of the world's surface area, but include 65 percent of its population. Almost half of the 10/40 Window consists of North Africa and Arabia, where Islam is the dominant religion. Over 90 percent of the world's poorest and most deprived, the children that are most abused, and most of the world's illiterate live in the window area.[39]

Consider this strategy and logic: Africa represents the Motherland to African Americans. African Americans have a natural cultural connection and closeness with Africans that Europeans do not share. Ethiopians (East Africans) have a natural cultural closeness with Arabians that Europeans and African Americans do not have. I believe African Americans are key to reaching North Africa. Likewise, I believe Ethiopians are key to reaching Arabia. Because of cultural barriers, African Americans may be more effective in reaching Africans than European Americans or Europeans. Ethiopians may be more effective at reaching Arabians than African Americans, European Americans, or Europeans.

In light of the September 11, 2001 terrorist attack on the World Trade Center Towers in New York City and subsequent events, it is evident that we are living in a new era.[40] Europeans and European Americans are becoming less welcome in many parts of the developing world. African Americans and Ethiopians are very important strategically to the fulfillment of God's missionary plan. A discussion of why Ethiopia is so special can be found in the book *Midnight Love Devotional.*[41] This work explores the calling God has placed on the African American Church and Ethiopia in this age. This is why the African American Cultural Center–*ETHIOPIA!* project is so important and worthy of support.

The official organizational name for the project is the Crystal Fountain Culture and Vision Center of Reconciliation (CFCAVCOR). The strategy of establishing CFCAVCOR is visionary. Perusal of the initial project proposal for CFCAVCOR demonstrates that the inspiration for the design and the foundation upon which this holistic project rests is the *missio Dei* (i.e., the mission of God).

CFCAVCOR
The Crystal Fountain Culture and
Vision Center of Reconciliation

The mission of the Crystal Fountain Culture and Vision Center of Reconciliation (CFCAVCOR) is to promote the mutually rich Christian heritage of African Americans and Ethiopians, vision and health care, community empowerment, cooperative economics and the ideas of reconciliation. CFCAVCOR will bridge the gap between cultures. This bridge will facilitate a dynamic and powerful exchange of art, science, commerce, and industry with significant cultural, political, and socioeconomic benefits. A predominating theme of the center will be ideas of reconciliation and cultural sensitivity with regional political stabilization in view. The Crystal Fountain Cultural and Vision Center of Reconciliation campus will have three clusters of operations: (1) the Cultural Center; (2) the Vocational Training and Vision Center; and (3) the HIV Center.

The Cultural Center will include museums (African American, Ethiopian), a library, and a human rights center. An archive will focus on the relations and similarities between the African people, especially Ethiopians, and African Americans from their arrival in the New World until the present day. It will facilitate creative and dynamic intellectual exchange of information, ideas, education, and the arts (e.g., visual, language, fashion, performance, food). This center will also be responsible for working with dignitaries involved in reconciliatory peace talks, coordinating activities related to those traveling to the center on spiritual pilgrimages, and overseeing programs connected with African American mobilization.

The Vocational Training and Vision Center will address the problems of poverty and illiteracy. Programs will focus on microenterprise development. Principles of cultural and gender sensitivity, civil rights, nonviolence, tolerance, and conflict resolution will be incorporated in community, youth, and prison reentry training programs.

The HIV Health Center will address the HIV/AIDS problem and house programs that focus on testing, education, counseling, and coordination with antiretroviral drugs and other treatment programs. Reconciliation counseling will be offered to infected individuals. HIV test-kit manufacturing and distribution will be included.

The underlying theme of CFCAVCOR is reconciliation and God's mission. The strategy is to demonstrate God's love in practical ways and elevate the Christian concept of reconciliation as demonstrated by Jesus Christ. Even though CFCAVCOR is not a religious corporation, unreached peoples who have not heard the Gospel message will see the Gospel message working in and through this organization. In other words, CFCAVCOR is a unique phenomenon, an organization and movement, a synergistic reunion of two powerful cultures, a living institution, a ssanctuary that speaks good tidings to all peoples, breathes God's peace, pronounces goodwill toward all peoples and out of which healing streams from the celestial Crystal Fountain flow! "God works in a mysterious way his wonders to perform."[42]

The key to connecting the African American church to God's mission is Africa. The key to connecting the African American church to Africa is Ethiopia. The institution of slavery in America robbed African Americans of their heritage. And slavery, the civil rights movement, and a few black inventions are the extent of what most Americans get exposed to about African American cultural heritage in public schools.

Ethiopia has a deep and rich biblical heritage, evidenced by the visit of the Queen of Sheba to King Solomon and the dynasty of kings in Ethiopia that resulted from them.[43] In fact, many scholars believe the original Ark of the Covenant to be in Ethiopia.[44] Ethiopia connects African American heritage not only to Africa but also to the Bible. Ethiopia, the only African nation to win the fight to protect its original religious and national heritage, represents the missing link to African American cultural heritage. This is the missing link that inquiring African American minds hunger and thirst for.

Ethiopia represents a link between Africa and Arabia. Ethiopians are both Semitic and Hamitic in their ancestry.[45] Not only is Ethiopia a door to Africa for the African American Church, but Ethiopia is also a door to the Middle East for the church. Ethiopian Christians are in the greatest position to reach unreached people groups in the Middle East not only because of common ancestry but also because Ethiopia and Ethiopians are held in high regard by the three major faith communities: Christianity, Judaism, and Islam.

The key to Ethiopians reaching the Middle East is the African American church. The African American church community can strengthen the Ethiopian church community, and the Ethiopian church community can strengthen the African American church community. The key to the African American church reaching both Africans and the Ethiopians is the great foundation that has already been laid by the large community of dedicated missionaries and mission-related organizations down through the years. All Christian communities must strategically work together synergistically for one common cause and purpose, God's mission. This is the strategy of CFCAVCOR.

CFCAVCOR, also known as the African American Cultural Center–*ETHIOPIA*! project, is to be an instrument of God to accomplish God's mission. In what we are calling "Operation Close the Window," CFCAVCOR will be instrumental in reaching the remaining unreached people groups within the 10/40 Window. The national sponsoring organization in Ethiopia for CFCAVCOR is Justice for All/PF Fellowship.[46]

As mentioned earlier, more information is available from the African American Center for World Mission (presentations to interested organizations, a one-day workshop) and the US Center for World Mission (books, literature, "Perspectives" course).

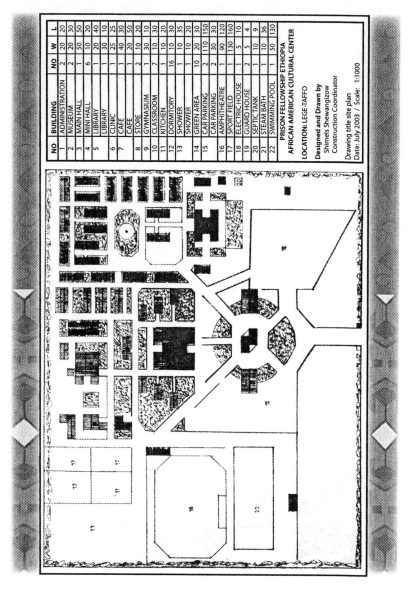

NO	BUILDING	NO	W	L
1	ADMINISTRATION	2	20	20
2	MUSEUM	2	20	30
3	MAIN HALL	1	50	50
4	MINI HALL	6	10	20
5	LIBRARY	1	20	40
	LIBRARY	1	30	10
6	CLINIC	1	25	25
7	CAFE	1	40	30
	CAFE	1	20	50
8	STORE	2	10	20
9	GYMNASIUM	1	30	10
10	CLASSROOM	7	10	30
11	KITCHEN	1	10	20
12	DORMITORY	16	10	30
13	SHOWER	1	10	35
	SHOWER	1	10	20
14	GREEN AREA	10	20	30
15	CAR PARKING	2	110	150
	CAR PARKING	2	30	30
16	AMPHITHEATRE	1	90	120
17	SPORT FIELD	1	130	160
18	ELECTRIC HOUSE	1	5	10
19	GUARD HOUSE	2	5	4
20	SEPTIC TANK	1	10	9
21	STEAM BATH	1	10	36
22	SWIMMING POOL	1	50	130

PRISON FELLOWSHIP ETHIOPIA
AFRICAN AMERICAN CULTURAL CENTER

LOCATION: LEGE-TAFFO

Designed and Drawn by
Shimels Shewangizow
Construction Coordinator

Drawing title site plan
Date: July 2003 / Scale: 1:1000

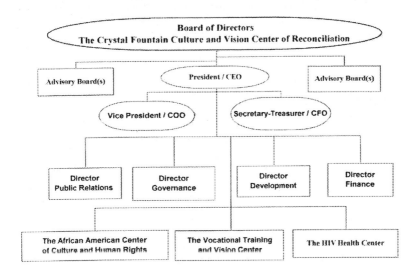

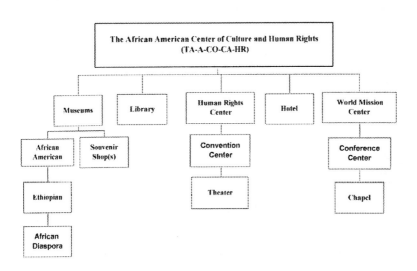

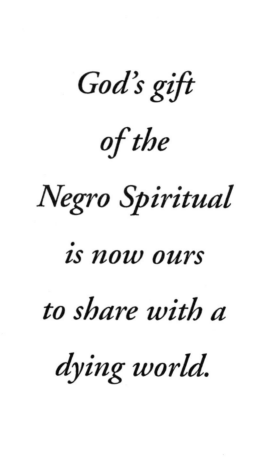

God's gift
of the
Negro Spiritual
is now ours
to share with a
dying world.

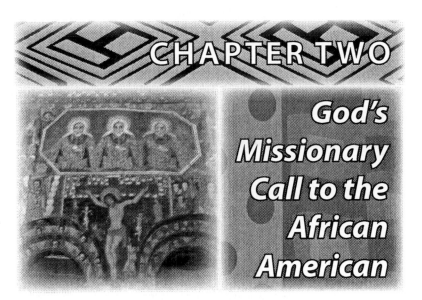

CHAPTER TWO

God's Missionary Call to the African American

The queen of the South will rise up.... (Luke 11:31, NKJV)

PEN YOUR EYES, AND YOU WILL SEE THAT WE ARE living through one of the transforming moments in the history of religion worldwide.[1] Over the past five centuries or so the story of Christianity has been inseparably bound up with that of Europe and European-derived civilizations overseas, above all in North America.[2] Recently, the overwhelming majority of Christians have lived in white nations, allowing theorists to speak smugly, even arrogantly, of European Christian civilization and Western imperialism.[3]

Over the past century, however, the center of gravity in the Christian world has shifted southward to Africa, Asia, and Latin America. Already the largest Christian communities on the planet are to be found in Africa and Latin America.[4] The era of Western Christianity has passed, and the day of Southern Christiandom is dawning! The idea of Christianity literally "going south" is not unfamiliar to religious studies scholars.[5]

Very soon, the two main centers of Christianity will be Africa and Latin America, but currently there is no common sense of identity that unites the church and believers of the two continents. For many Protestant Africans, the World Council of Churches offers a major institutional focus of unity, but because the Roman Catholic Church abstains from membership in the council, this forum is closed to the majority of Latin Americans. Professor Philip Jenkins reports:

> The resulting segregation of interests and ideas is remarkable, since the churches in Africa and Latin America share so many common experiences. They are passing through similar phases of growth, and are, independently, developing similar social and theological worldviews. Both also face similar issues, of race, of enculturation, of just how to deal with their respective colonial heritages. All these are common hemispheric issues that fundamentally separate the experiences of Northern and Southern churches. Given the lively scholarly activity and the flourishing spiritually in both Africa and Latin America, a period of mutual discovery is inevitable. When it begins—when, not if—the interaction should launch a revolutionary new era in world religion. Although many see the process of globalization as yet another form of American imperialism, it would be ironic if an early consequence was a growing sense of identity between Southern Christians. Once that axis is established, we really would be speaking of a new Christendom, based in the Southern Hemisphere.[6]

African Americans have a special and essential role to play in God's missionary plan as we approach the end of the church age and the fulfillment of global evangelism. The Crystal Fountain

Culture and Vision Center of Reconciliation (CFCAVCOR) in Addis Ababa, Ethiopia, will mobilize the African American church and help secure the connection between Latin American and African churches in the new Southern Christendom. Brazil, with one of the world's largest populations of Africans in the diaspora, will play a major role in this regard.

As Christianity moves south, it is in some ways returning to its roots. Founded in the Near East, Christianity for its first thousand years was stronger in Asia and North Africa than in Europe, and only after about A.D. 1400 did Europe (and subsequently, Europeanized North America) decisively become the Christian heartland.[7] This account challenges the oddly prevalent view of Christianity as a white or Western ideology foisted on the rest of an unwilling globe by such means as Spanish galleons, British redcoats, and American televangelists.[8]

Many Black Muslims in America reject Christianity because of the incorrect belief and perception that Christianity is a white man's religion. Jenkins comments on this faulty picture and image of Christianity:

> In this popular image, Christianity becomes not just an aspect of Western imperialism, but an essential justification for that whole era. When twentieth-century African Americans sought religious roots distinct from the mainstream culture that spurned them, a substantial minority opted for the Muslim faith, which they regarded as authentically African. Christianity, in contrast, was seen as the tool of the slave-masters. (Few Westerners pay any attention to the long history of Arab Muslim slaving enterprises in Africa.) As "everyone knows," the authentic religions of Africa and Asia are faiths like Hinduism, Buddhism, animism, and above all, Islam. Not just among Blacks, a common assumption holds that when we do find Christianity outside the West, it must have been brought there from the West, probably in the past century or two. Images of Victorian missionaries' pith helmets are commonly in the background.
>
> The power of this hostile picture is all the more surprising when we realize how easily available are the historical sources and modern scholarly studies that utterly contradict it. We do not have to excavate obscure scholarly collections in order to read the rich and ancient histories of African and Asian Christianity. Based on this very large literature, we can see that at no point did the West have a monopoly on the Christian faith. And even at the height of the missionary endeavor, non-Western converts very soon absorbed and adopted the religion according to their own cultural needs.[9]

Jenkins, author of *The Next Christendom*, has noted, "Apart from Egypt, much early Christian history focuses on the Roman province known as Africa, roughly modern Tunisia. This was the home of such great leaders as Tertullian, Cyprian, and Augustine, the founders of Christian Latin literature."[10]

It is often thought that not only Christianity but civilization itself came from Europe. Nothing can be further from the truth.

> Rome got her civilization from Greece; Greece borrowed hers from Egypt, thence she'd derived her science and beautiful mythology. Civilization descended the Nile and spread over the delta, as it came down from Thebes. Thebes was built and settled by the Ethiopians. As we ascend the Nile we come to Meroe, the queen city of Ethiopia and the cradle of learning into which all Africa poured its caravans. So we trace the light of civilization from Ethiopia to Egypt, to Greece, to Rome, and thence diffusing its radiance over the entire world.[11]

In the earliest periods of history, the Ethiopians attained a high degree of civilization and became one of the world's first and oldest Christian nations. The Ethiopian church is ancient, and the book of Acts records that one of the first Gentile converts was an Ethiopian court official (Acts 8:26-40). By the time the first Anglo-Saxons were converted, Ethiopian Christianity was already in its tenth generation.[12]

> Through the Middle Ages, the symbolic center of the Christian kingdom was at the ancient capital of Aksum [Ethiopia], long a point of contact with Pharaonic Egypt. An Episcopal see was founded here around 340, and this remained the "home of the Ark of the Covenant, Ethiopia's original New Jerusalem." The Egyptian connection created a potent monastic tradition that endures to this day.[13]

While in Ethiopia, my son and I visited a Ethiopian Orthodox Tewahedo Church monk on the remote and ancient 'island' monastery of Tana Cherkos on Lake Tana. This is the place where the Ark is claimed to have been hidden for close to one thousand years. The monk claimed not only that the Ark of the Covenant was initially brought to this monastery but also that Mary, Joseph, and baby Jesus visited the Ark there during the time the angel told them to leave Bethlehem for Egypt. This information is considered legend and cannot be proven one way or another.[14]

Although scarcely known by Westerners, the Ethiopian church offers one of the most heroic success stories in Christianity of defending the faith and their Christian nation from invasion and colonization. Not only is Ethiopia the oldest Christian nation in the world, but it is the only African country that has never been colonized (Liberia is regarded as colonized by the American Colonization Society).

> Ethiopia's prestige in Africa consequent upon her triumphant success in repelling invasion, and in having remained unconquered throughout the centuries, is practically unfathomable. To the Africans in general, not only to those who invoked her as a liberator, she stands as granite monument, a living exponent and testimony of the innate puissance of the black race, the shrine enclosing the last sacred resistance against white invasion, a living symbol, an incarnation of African independence.[15]

The Ethiopian church does have some idiosyncrasies. But it would be a daring outsider who would suggest that the faith for which Ethiopians have struggled and died over 1,700 years is anything less than a pure manifestation of the Christian tradition.[16]

The African American church has a very important role to play in God's unfolding mission plan. Most of the unreached peoples in the world live in the 10/40 Window, half of which consists of North Africa and Arabia. The African American church is key to evangelizing North Africa. The African American church is key to mobilizing Ethiopian missionaries to Arabia. The African American church may also be key to connecting the South American church with the African church by way of Brazil, with its large black population. Brazil and Ethiopia will be leaders in the new Southern Christendom. The mobilization of African American missionaries and the establishment of the African American Cultural Center— *ETHIOPIA*! project may prove to be crucial components in the unfolding drama of God's missionary plan and present a new paradigm for the African American church.

A CRUCIAL CROSSROADS

The African American church is at a crossroads. For many years, the African American church has been deeply involved in making a dream, which sparked the Civil Rights movement in America, come true. Because most of the world is aware of our plight in America—our struggle from slavery to civil rights—

many want to hear our story and how our God delivered us from oppression. African American missionaries have a great opportunity to minister to the peoples of the world. Our dark skin, which used to be viewed as a curse, is now known to be a blessing for spreading the Gospel message. God moves in mysterious ways! God's gift of the Negro spiritual helped African Americans deal with the institution of slavery, and now that same gift is ours to share with a dying world.[17]

The Reverend Dr. Martin Luther King Jr.'s dream of basic equal human rights for all humans has been realized in America to a large degree, and now the African American church has to decide at what level of involvement, if any, it should continue in the pursuit of the next level of the American Dream—obtaining socioeconomic parity. In many churches in America there has been a dangerous drift toward unbalanced promotion of wealth and prosperity with the aim of pursuing lifestyles of the rich and famous. Because of the current American culture, the danger for the African American church is that an unfocused and diverse pursuit of socioeconomic parity may in fact become a collective descent to hedonism and self-destruction. There is more to life than material wealth. Preaching of the whole counsel of God is being replaced in many churches with a different Gospel, a watered-down message that lacks the power of God. However, the pursuit of socioeconomic parity with emphasis on uniting African American resources and efforts to bring mission support and aid our homeland *is* powerful because it is in line with God's mission.

African American pastors must decide which road to travel. The African American pastor, with socioeconomic parity in view, must choose whether to lead God's flock to pursue the lifestyles of the rich and famous or to fall in line with the Good

Shepherd and, like a faithful undershepherd, pursue God's heart for the unreached peoples of the world! I am afraid too many pastors have lost focus. I'm afraid the focus and repeat conversation of many pastors has drifted to the "How many?" and "How much?" Are we pursuing the lifestyles of the rich and famous or God's mission? Which is first? Have we become the servants of the gospel of prosperity or the Gospel of Jesus Christ? Are we faithfully serving the God who called us into his service? Are we preaching the full counsel of God?

My father, the Reverend Leon Johnson of Evanston, Illinois, is a great man. He reminds us that Noah was given eight members to start his church, and 120 years later when the flood came he still had only eight members in his church. He had the same eight family members. Yet God rewarded Noah and listed his name in the Faith Hall of Fame (Hebrews 11:7). God honored

Noah not because he started with eight members and ended up with "many" members and "much" personal wealth but rather because he was faithful with what God gave him and what God told him to do. Noah believed God and was obedient to God's command.

God honors us when we believe him and obey him. Let's stop asking, "How many you running?" and "How much you got?" Let's stop asking, "How many revivals you doing?" and "How much you getting paid?" Let's start asking each other about the African American church and God's missionary call. Or better yet, let's just flip the switch. Somehow our focus has gotten twisted. God wants us to regroup and refocus and get this thing right. Let us start asking the question in a different way. Let's ask, "How many local missionaries are you sending out?" and "How much are you putting in your mission budget?"

African American pastors who are heavily involved in local socioeconomic and political parity efforts must also believe that God has a heart for all unreached people groups in the world. They must also obey God's command that his priority of global mission becomes theirs. God is recruiting African American missionaries from all over the country to join a new army that will usher in the unfolding drama of the coming of the Kingdom of Heaven. They are coming from every state, every county, every city and municipality. They are in your church. Are you one of them? Are you a soldier in the army of the Lord? Jesus tells us to be his witnesses starting in Jerusalem, then Judea and Samaria and to the end of the earth (Acts 1:8). Could Ethiopia be our Jerusalem? Is Jesus calling us to Ethiopia, then Africa and Arabia, and to the end of the earth?

Life is about God's agenda. Whose agenda are we following? "This gospel of the kingdom will be preached in all the world as a witness to all the nations, and then the end will come" (Matthew 24:14, NKJV). This passage explains God's agenda and God's priority, God's mission!

It is the calling of every Christian to use what God has given us, blessed us with, to be a blessing to others—to the glory of God! It is time for the African American church to share with the world the many riches of God's manifold blessings bestowed upon us. It is time for the African American church to play its unique and crucial role in God's missionary plan, in God's purpose to bless the nations.

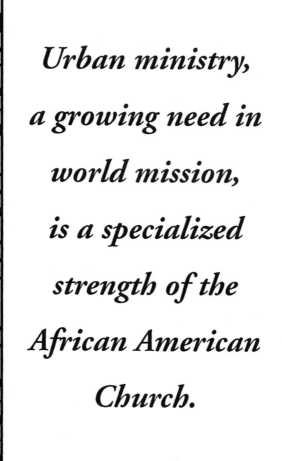

*Urban ministry,
a growing need in
world mission,
is a specialized
strength of the
African American
Church.*

CHAPTER THREE

Local Mission Ministry

For I was hungry and you gave Me food; I was thirsty and you gave Me drink;
I was a stranger and you took Me in; I was naked and you clothed Me;
I was sick and you visited Me; I was in prison an you came to Me.
(Matthew 25:35-36 NKJV)

HE AFRICAN AMERICAN CHURCH HAS DONE, AND continues to do, great things in the area of local mission ministry. In fact, most of what the African American Church has done in the past century in missions falls under the banner of urban ministry. The high level of sophistication in the area of urban ministry is evidenced in many African American churches by the presence of the various ministries listed below.

◆ Food bank (food distribution to the hungry)

◆ Clothing bank (new/used clothing distribution to the needy)

◆ Job training/preparation programs

◆ Entrepreneur training

◆ Computer lab/computer training/applications

◆ Street evangelism

◆ Activities for local evangelism (such as block parties)

◆ Substance abuse support groups (support groups for substance abuse abatement.)

◆ Seminars on interviewing techniques, filling the job application, developing resume.

◆ Test taking skills/college prep (enhancement school/ training for assistance in taking tests for job application, schools.)

◆ Financial counseling (counseling for those continue to ask the church for financial assistance, those who are in financial distress with credit cares bills, general money management.)

◆ Re-entry programs (assisting ex-prisoners reenter society as productive citizens. Coordinates with other ministries of the church.)

◆ Prison ministry (going into prisons/jails to do ministry. Helping family members who have members in prison with visitation; assist with prisoner and prisoner family needs.)

◆ Youth intervention programs

◆ Mentorship programs, after school programs, counseling and activities.

◆ Emergency housing

◆ Utility and other emergency assistance.

◆ Disaster relief (Working with Red Cross or other agencies in disaster relief)

◆ Immigration Assistance (Assisting those coming to this country to get settled.)

English as Second Language (Educational classes to help foreigners learn English language. Assist them in getting enrolled in schools that offer this service.)

Single Parents

Support groups for various needs.

Health and HIV ministry (assist with HIV education, testing, and referral services. Coordinate needs with other resource agencies)

Transportation assistance (to church, doctor and other emergency needs).

Bereavement (assist with the needs of bereaved families. Information regarding burials issues, etc.)

Senior citizens' programming

Distribution of information on affordable housing and other special services.

Sick and shut-in (visitation of the sick and shut-in.)

Mission Activity:

Fifth Sundays, women in white, good deeds?

Given that these kinds of ministries are typical of African American churches, much of the activity of the churches can be viewed from a missionary perspective: however, most of what the church has done under the banner of missionary work has been local missions, that is, urban community-based mission ministry. Often, in many African American churches, the word "missions" in the mind of the average church member is associated in an even more restrictive manner and scope. Research surveys done at the African American Center for World Mission suggest that most members of African American churches understand missions not as cross-cultural missions participation but as home missions activities.[1]

In traditional African American churches, mission activity is often associated with taking money from a church mission fund to help a church member pay a bill. Mission activity in many traditional African American churches is also often associated with a celebration on fifth Sundays by women dressed in white who do good deeds in the church.

Urban community-based mission ministry is a specialized strength of the African American Church. Urban mission ministry is a growing need in world mission. God's missionary plan extends beyond our immediate communities. God's call to the African American Church to global missions is becoming more pronounced and audible to a growing number of African Americans around the country as God's missionary plan draws to an end.

Can you hear God calling you to help Him fulfill His missionary plan? We have entered End Time ministry. The world is changing. Times are different. Will the African American Church take the right road in these changing times and partner with God to accomplish God's global missionary plan?

Date 2/4/04
No. 301/ZA/04

የኢትዮጵያ ቆንስላ ጀኔራል ጽ/ቤት
ሎስ አንጀለስ
CONSULATE GENERAL OF ETHIOPIA
LOS ANGELES

Dr. Leonidas A. Johnson
President
Crystal Fountain Ministries, Inc.
Diamond Bar, CA 91765

Dear Dr. Johnson

Thank you for taking time out of your busy schedule to come to the Consulate General of Ethiopia and discuss about your plan for establishing the African American Cultural and Vision Center of reconciliation in Ethiopia.

The Consulate General of Ethiopia is very much in support of your plan and look forward for its implementation. It is also the desire of the Consulate General to help in facilitating to establish the center that will tremendously contribute in the exchange of culture, education, science, trade and investment between the people of Ethiopia and the United States of America.

The Consulate General wishes the best in your endeavors

Respectfully,

[signature]

Thye Atske Selassie
Consul General

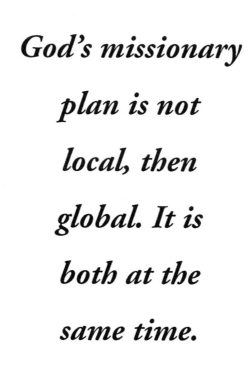

God's missionary plan is not local, then global. It is both at the same time.

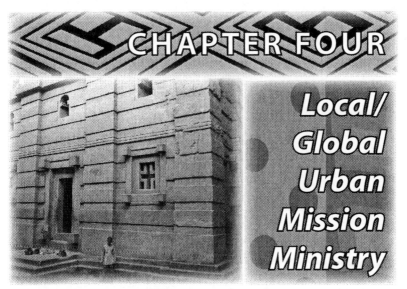

CHAPTER FOUR

Local/ Global Urban Mission Ministry

…A man of Macedonia stood and pleaded with him, saying, "Come over to Macedonia and help us." (Acts 16:9 NKJV)

S WE HAVE SEEN, MUCH OF THE ACTIVITY OF African American churches can be viewed from a missionary perspective. However, most of what the church has done under the banner of missionary work has been local mission—that is, urban community-based mission ministry. But what about global mission?

God is a missionary God, and the purpose of the church is to fulfill his missionary plan. God is not vague about what his mission is. God wants the church to make disciples within every people group. But how will this ever happen if the African American church only concentrates on home and its immediate urban communities? The hungry and poor will always be with us. God's mission is not simply to help poor or needy people. We do not have to go to Africa to find poor and needy people; we can find them in our families, in our neighborhoods, in our communities!

God's missionary plan is for the church to evangelize every ethnic community in the world and establish an indigenous church movement in that community to evangelize and disciple that people. God wants us to establish an indigenous, self-sustaining church movement within every people group so that new converts may come and be discipled in their own language, in their own church, and by people of their own culture! This is the primary purpose of the church, and the African American church has an important role to play.

God's missionary plan is not local, then global. It is not one first, then the other. It's not linear, but circular; it's both at the same time. As the Rev. Kwesi Kamau put it simply at the fortieth anniversary celebration of the National Black Evangelical Association, "Missions is local and global."[1] It's time for the African American church to take what we *know* to where God wants us to *go*!

Jesus did not tell the disciples to start to minister in their own community first then branch out. The disciples were not from Jerusalem; they were from Galilee. Jesus told them to go to Jerusalem and start there. We have it wrong when we cite Jesus' command to start in Jerusalem and go out from there as proof that we must start in our own communities before branching out. We must go where Jesus tells us to go. It very well may be that God is telling us to start in our Jerusalem—Ethiopia—and from there branch out.

Let's take what we *know* to where God wants us to *go*.

Well, what about our own local communities? Yes, we must minister to our local communities and minister where Jesus tells us to go. Jesus is the man with the plan. We must direct our steps and walk in the paths that he has prepared for us to travel. It's time for the African American church to wake up and take what we *know* to where God wants us to *go*!

Only a few global missionaries from the United States are African American. Even though African Americans make up some 12 percent of the US population, less than 1 percent of the US mission force is African American, according to the Rev. Ivor Duberry.[2] Even though African Americans have not been present in cross-cultural world mission in large numbers over the past hundred years, African Americans are specially equipped for world mission, especially because of the atrocious experiences of overcoming oppression in America which heightened our sensitivity to issues of discrimination, segregation, racism, and the political and socioeconomic dynamics of the civil rights movement.

Another important reason why African Americans are specially equipped for world mission is that the African American church has become very adept in urban ministry. United Nations projections suggest that most of the global population growth in the coming decades will be urban. Today, around 45 percent of the world's people live in urban areas, but that proportion should rise to 60 percent by 2025 and to more than 66 percent by 2050.[3]

> In 1900, all the world's largest cities were located in either Europe or North America. Today, only three of the world's ten largest urban areas can be found in traditionally advanced countries, namely Tokyo, New York City, and Los Angeles, and by 2015, the only one of these names left on the list will be Tokyo…. Currently, 80 percent of the world's largest urban conglomerations are located in either Asia or Latin America, but African cities will become much more significant by mid-century. The proportion of Africans living in urban areas will grow from around 40 percent today to almost 66 percent by 2050. Rich pickings await any religious groups who can meet the needs of these new urbanites, anyone who can at once feed the body and nourish the soul.[4]

Even though much global ministry will involve urban ministry, there is and will continue to be ample need for rural ministry. The idea of global ministry to rural areas is a goal of the Cooperative Mission Network of the African Dispersion's (COMINAD) Adopt-a-Village ministry.[5] The mission of COMINAD is to mobilize Christian descendents of Africa to do cross-cultural missions especially among unreached people groups. Their Adopt-A-Village ministry is a project designed to build relationships between villages in Africa and churches in the West.

Is the African American church ready, willing and able to meet God's challenge? It is time for the African American church to wake up! Get up out the bed and arise from your slumber, Black Giant, and march on into new territories to do what we know we can do, what God has prepared us to do, and what we already have done in America? It is time for the African American church to take our local missions ministries global. This is the dawning of a new age. God is calling the

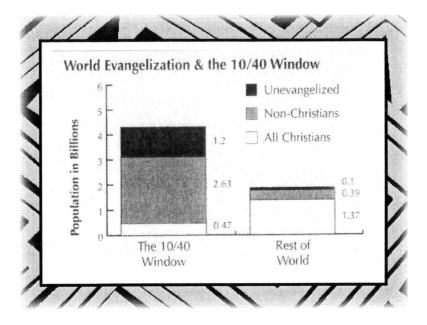

African American church to meet the challenge. The African American church is most suited for reaching many unreached people groups in North Africa. I believe the African American church is God's battle-axe—God's instrument to destroy one of the last citadels of satanic power and strongholds left in this world (cf. Jeremiah 51:20).

Africa is one of the last remaining frontiers in God's missionary plan to gather a remnant within each of the world's people groups. It's time, it's time, it's time! It's time for the African American church to take what we *know* where God has prepared a path for us to go! Let's do this thing!

Missions committees should affirm ongoing ministry activities as local missions but also stress possible applications for global missions.

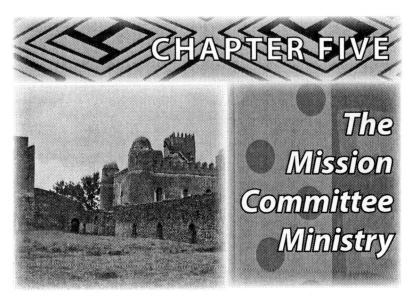

CHAPTER FIVE

The Mission Committee Ministry

*Having then gifts differing according to the grace that is given to us,
let us use them.... (Romans 12:6, NKJV)*

T IS IMPORTANT TO RECOGNIZE THAT WORKING AS a committee is one of the most effective ways of accomplishing work in the church.[1] *Committee* may be an outdated term, but it represents the small group or leadership team that functions as a group to insure that certain tasks of the church get done.

Standard officers of the committee would include president, vice president, secretary, treasurer, and chaplain. Subcommittees may be formed to coordinate local mission and global mission. Since the church is a missionary instrument of God for global mission, it is essential that the pastor, minister of education, and other key leaders be actively involved with the missions committee.

Jesus established the church as an instrument to complete God's mission. Mission is not a part of the church; rather, the church is a part of God's mission.[2] Let us understand mission according to God's revelation of what mission is all about. The pastor will rely on the mission committee to help the congregation make the paradigm shift in thinking from a local urban/community ministry mind-set to a global urban/community mission mind-set. Helping the congregation make this paradigm shift is a vital function of the mission committee.

It is important for any mission committee to recognize the many ministries of the church that are currently doing the work of missions on a local level. It will not be necessary for the mission committee to do the home missions-related activities of the local church or to take over what another ministry is already doing or is charged to do. Rather, the committee should recognize the various mission ministry activities under way, note them and educate the church body that these ministries fall under the rubric of local mission but that the same activities could also be part of global mission. The logistical details of certain urban ministries may help the committee facilitate global mission. For example, elements of how a church operates its local clothing ministry may also be appropriate in an overseas setting.

Local Mission Coordinator

The local mission coordinator's primary objective may include organizing reports of the various activities of the church with regard to local urban mission ministry. Since much of what the church does may be considered missions work, it is not the role of the mission committee to *take over* any existing ministry; but rather to *work with* that ministry. Other church ministries and committees should be encouraged to communicate with the mission committee regarding the various mission-related activities. The local mission coordinator will act as a liaison between the local urban mission ministry and the global mission ministry efforts.

A secondary responsibility for the local coordinator may include generally encouraging members involved in local ministry to get involved in global mission ministry. An initial phase might be to get these workers involved in similar types of urban ministry in other cities, churches, or locations. This will help workers get accustomed to travel and experiencing like ministry in different places. The next step might be a short-term mission trip overseas. It is important to identify members working in mission ministry as possible candidates for short-term mission trips and even long-term, cross-cultural mission service.

Whereas most local mission-related activities will be done by other church ministries, most of the global mission activities will be directly coordinated and administered by the mission committee.

Global Mission Coordinator

Major subcommittees and activities of the global mission coordinator may include the work of the *goer* and the *sender* coordinators.

Goer Coordinator

Goers are those who actually go on cross-cultural mission fields, either as short-term or career missionaries. The main duties of the goer coordinator include recruiting and mobilizing missionaries

> # Many resources and tools can ease entry into this new age of global ministry.

and teams to go on specific trips and/or assignments. More important, though, the goer coordinator would be responsible to assist with the mental, physical, and spiritual preparation for specific assignments. This may include the sponsorship of specific educational seminars and briefings for the missionaries and team members that are preparing to go on specific trips or assignments. This coordinator must work closely with the local mission coordinator in recruitment efforts and in coordinating local/global urban mission ministry strategies and efforts for specific mission trips. The Goer coordinator will often travel with and give leadership to the mission team on mission trips.

Sender Coordinator

Responsibilities for the sender coordinator may include all logistical support for the goers. Logistical support includes gathering necessary information and documentation for the various trips (insurance, visa, passport, immunizations, etc.). Responsibilities may also include prayer support and communications while on mission, welcoming missionaries home upon their return, and helping with the debriefing process. Sender coordinator responsibilities may also include developing opportunities for the returning missionaries to share their experiences with others.

Budget considerations will vary from church to church, but budget items for the mission committee should be distinguished between local mission and global mission ministry. The local mission ministry budget should comprise the separate individual budgets for each local church ministry. Each local church ministry should allocate time, talent, and treasure toward some type of mission activity or project and report this to the local mission coordinator. Data on monies spent for local church mission ministries should be collected for information and educational purposes. The global mission ministry budget should focus on God's global missionary call to the church. Considerations should include funding the team leader for short-term mission trips along with the necessary equipment for the documentation of the trip and presentations of photographs and other information upon return. Funds should also be set aside to support missionaries serving full-time on the global mission field. It would be best to look at the overall church budget and set aside a percentage for global mission.

There are other models for establishing a mission committee in your church. For example, the Rev. Ivor Duberry has proposed a missions program that can be modified for a particular church's dynamics.[3] Also, the Rev. Dr. Jim Sutherland of Reconciliation Ministry Network (Chattanooga, Tennessee) has a mission team manual and other helpful African American mission resource materials accessible on the Internet that would be helpful in establishing a mission ministry.[4] These resources and tools are merely suggestions to aid you as God leads and directs your entry into this new age of mission ministry for the African American church.

And this gospel of the kingdom will be preached in all the world as a witness to all the nations, and then the end will come (Matthew 24:14).

CHAPTER SIX

The Black Giant: A Charge to the African American Church

Matthew 24:14; Psalms 107:13-16; 102:18-22; 66:10-12; Matthew 24:3-14

PROLEGOMENA

 REETINGS IN THE NAME OF OUR LORD AND SAVIOR Jesus Christ. All praises to God who is the head of my life. To the pastor of this church, officers, members, visitors, and special guests, it is a joy and pleasure for me to present unto you a word from the Lord.

It is my duty to inform you that the wages of sin is death, and though it may be true that all have sinned and fall short of the glory of God, it is equally true that the gift of God is eternal life through faith in Jesus Christ (cf. Romans 6:23; 3:23). It is my job to help open your eyes in order to turn you from darkness to light, from the power of Satan to God, that you may receive forgiveness of sins and an inheritance among those who are sanctified by faith in Jesus Christ (cf. Acts 26:18). Have you not read, have you not heard, the devil is a liar; the promises of God are true!

The background texts for this sermon are found in Psalm 107:13-16; 102:18-22; 66:10-12 and Matthew 24:3-14. There you will find these words:

> *Then they cried out to the Lord in their trouble, and He saved them out of their distresses. He brought them out of darkness and the shadow of death, and broke their chains in pieces. Oh, that men would give thanks to the LORD for His goodness, and for His wonderful works to the children of men! For He has broken the gates of bronze, and cut the bars of iron in two. (Psalm 107:13-16)*

• • • • • •

> *This will be written for the generation to come, that a people yet to be created may praise the LORD. For He looked down from the height of His sanctuary; from heaven the LORD viewed the earth, to hear the groaning of the prisoner, to release those appointed to death, to declare the name of the LORD in Zion, and His praise in Jerusalem, when the peoples are gathered together, and the kingdoms, to serve the Lord. (Psalm 102:18-22)*

• • • • • •

> *For you, O God, have tested us; You have refined us as silver is refined. You brought us into the net; You laid affliction on our backs. You have caused men to ride over our heads; we went through fire and through water; but You brought us out to rich fulfillment. (Psalm 66:10-12)*

• • • • • •

> *Now as He sat on the Mount of Olives, the disciples came to Him privately, saying, "Tell us, when will these things be? And what will be the sign of Your coming, and of the end of the age?" And Jesus answered and said to them: "Take heed*

that no one deceives you. For many will come in my name, saying, 'I am the Christ,' and will deceive many. And you will hear of wars and rumors of wars. See that you are not troubled; for all these things must come to pass, but the end is not yet. For nation will rise against nation, and kingdom against kingdom. And there will be famines, pestilences, and earthquakes in various places. All these are the beginning of sorrows. Then they will deliver you up to tribulation and kill you, and you will be hated by all nations for My name's sake. And then many will be offended, will betray one another, and will hate one another. Then many false prophets will rise up and deceive many. And because lawlessness will abound, the love of many will grow cold. But he who endures to the end shall be saved. And this gospel of the kingdom will be preached in all the world as a witness to all the nations, and then the end will come." (Matthew 24:3-14 NKJV)

• • • • • •

Our key text is Matthew 24:14:

And this gospel of the kingdom will be preached in all the world as a witness to all the nations, and then the end will come.

The title of this sermon is "The Black Giant."

PRAYER

Father, open now the Crystal Fountain whence Thy healing stream does flow. Bread of Heaven, feed us until we want no more. Let whosoever thirst come and whosoever will, let them take the water of life freely. Satan, I am an ambassador for Christ; by the authority Jesus has invested in me I hereby rebuke you in the name of Jesus Christ. Father, may the seeds planted from this message bear much fruit and bring salvation and glory to Your name.

INTRODUCTION

Yo Ho Ho! Black Giant. I want to tell you a story about a giant. Yo Ho Ho Ho Ho! A real giant. Yo Ho Ho Ho Ho! A sleeping giant! Yo Ho Ho Ho Ho! A black giant! This is no ordinary

story, as you will soon see. In fact, it is part of the greatest story every told. To help illustrate the wonder and magnificence of this true story, I will employ the use of a fictitious story about a boy named Leo.

STORY

Once upon a time in a land of lions, kings, and queens, a land renowned in the ancient world for its magnificent architectural structures and libraries, a land full of wisdom and knowledge, a land abounding in science and industry, a land full of beautiful exotic tropical gardens, a land filled with gold and ivory, a land over flowing with milk and honey, a land where God walked in the cool of the day, a land of paradise, a land kissed by the rays of the beautiful sun, a land where no one is wronged, a cultural Mecca and reservoir of history whose fame spread throughout the known world, in this cradle of humanity there lived a boy by the name of Leo. His grandfather called him the Lion of Ham, but most people just called him Leo.

Leo was the first-born son of King Ham, the son of King Nimrod. Leo was healthy, wealthy, and wise. He was a handsome brave hunter and had the makings of a strong leader. Leo lived in a village with his brothers, sisters, cousins, aunts, uncles, parents, grandparents, great grandparents, and friends.

One day Leo woke up early. He was so excited about the upcoming ceremony and celebration that he could hardly stand it. As he tossed and turned, he said to himself, "I will arise and go gather fresh coffee beans, tea leaves, and bananas for today's celebration." In no time flat he was gathering berries in his favorite spot, when all of a sudden, as the sun peeked over the horizon, he was snatched, gagged, blindfolded, tied up and led captive by strangers. Leo fought courageously. "Help!" He called for help, but the sound of his voice was muffled.

Leo was beaten with a stick until he was violently swallowed up in a bloody pool of pain, darkness, and despair. When he awoke, he found himself bound, shackled in chains, and lying in a dark, damp, smelly place. Days turned into weeks.

Finally he was herded into a boat. "There are too many people in this boat," he thought. There was no room to sit or even stand. Leo lay crammed in shoulder to shoulder with hundreds of other tired, hungry, injured, sick, and bewildered boys and girls. The boat rocked and rolled. The hunger, the sickness was more than most could bear. Many died, and their bodies were fed to ferocious sharks. Others were sacrificed to these man eating sea creatures while yet alive.

At first Leo couldn't believe such a thing could happen, but he soon realized this was no dream. He got angry until his anger caused his stomach to hurt. He prayed, "Lord, help me, save me." Leo didn't want to cry, he tried not to, but he could not hold it back any longer, he cried and cried until he had no more tears. Grief and sorrow were his constant companions. He felt trapped in a time warp, bound by problems; depression had gotten Leo down. He was losing his grip on hope. Despair was starting to settle in. Leo didn't think that he would see the blue sky, dry land, his family, or his home ever again.

FIRST CALL
(CALL-AND-RESPONSE—CALL FOR BUY-IN)

I wonder if anybody here knows anything about being bound and shackled with problems? Anybody here know anything about drowning in depression? Don't tell me I'm the only one. Anybody know what it is like to come to the end of your rope? Anybody here been victimized by circumstances beyond your control? No wealth, poor health, this thing happened, that thing happened, and all of a sudden everything starts changing, and things go from bad to worse. Seems like the whole world is against you.

Tell me, how does it feel? No, I'll tell you how it feels; let me put it this way, it don't feel good. It makes you mad and sad, and if you don't handle it right, it will make you lose control and lose your mind, and that's bad. That's how Leo felt, but God looked down from heaven, bowed His ear, and heard Leo's despairing cry and pitied his every groan.

BIBLE/HISTORY

The Bible says God is a God that looks down from the height of His sanctuary; from heaven the Lord views the earth to hear the groaning of the prisoner. History tells us that Africans were violently taken prisoner from their homes in Africa and enslaved in places like the West Indies, Brazil, and North America. Just as the Israelites were afflicted in Egypt by mean ol' Pharaoh and his powerful army four hundred years, Europeans in America afflicted African Americans for almost four hundred years. Yes, God heard the cries of the Israelites and sent Moses to tell mean ol' Pharaoh, thus says the Lord: "Let My people go." Go down, Moses, tell ol' Pharaoh to let My people go. Yes, God heard the cries of the African American.

In the words of Charles H. Wesley:

> Between 1500 and 1850 close to fourteen million slaves were imported throughout the Americas...The Privy Council estimated that 4.5 per cent of the slaves died waiting in the harbor to be sold, 13 per cent during the trip to America, and 33 per cent died while being seasoned in the West Indies. According to these figures, only 50 per cent of the Africans survived to work as slaves throughout the New World.[1]

Yes, God heard, and God delivered these precious people, this peculiar treasure, African Americans from the hand of slavery, lynching, segregation, discrimination, and prejudice. Yes, God delivered African Americans out of the horrible pit of social, political, and economic oppression. Even though racism still lives, racism does not rule. Yes, affliction was laid on our backs. Many African Americans suffered and died horrible deaths in the fight for basic human rights. Yes, there were many gruesome atrocities and heart-wrenching casualties in the "nonviolent" civil rights movement. Yes, the descendants of Japheth have ridden over our heads. Yes, the descendants of Ham went through fire and through water. But God, I say, but God has brought us out to rich fulfillment. Amen! Just as the Hebrews left Egypt with riches from Egypt, so shall the African American church send forth missionaries with riches from the most technologically rich and prosperous nation in the world unto Africa, Arabia, and Asia.

STORY

Back to Leo. The last we heard of Leo, he was sinking in the muddy and swampy quagmires of depression. Mad and sad, things were getting bad. One day, after many weeks of journey across the ocean, the ship started a-rocking and a-rolling like never before. Leo could hear the winds howling like hyenas and the thunder booming louder than ten thousand lions. Lightning flashed brighter than the sun on an uncloudy day. The ship was tossed and driven and battered by an angry sea. In a flash all was lost. The ship, far from the peaceful shore, was sinking, sinking, sinking to rise no more.

But then the Master of the sea heard Leo's despairing cry. From the waters Leo was lifted, and he drifted safely to shore. Weakened and dehydrated, Leo lay half dead on the beach, still shackled to a remnant of the broken-up ship. How about that? That which once imprisoned him became his life preserver in the storm. That which men meant for evil God flipped the switch and used for good (cf. Genesis 50:20). My, my, my! Let me hear you say, "flip the switch." "God works in a mysterious way, His wonders to perform."[2]

As Leo lay still on the shore, people came to see such a sight, and such a sight it was. You see, Leo, the Lion of Ham, was not only darker then anybody they had ever seen, he was also like a giant to these people. At first they could not tell if he was dead or alive. The little people were afraid of this black giant and decided to tie him down with cords that could not be broken. The little people worked desperately to tie down the sleeping black giant. As Leo lay helpless, ropes were shot across his motionless body and tacked down with stakes. The little people lit a fire. They laughed, joked, and made fun of Leo, because Leo was not like them. Leo was different. This made many of the little folks uncomfortable and afraid. They thought and figured while Leo the Lion of Ham was down, they would do everything in their power to keep this black man down.

SECOND CALL (HISTORY/BIBLE)

You know, history tells us this very thing happened in America. African kings and queens, parents and children were hunted, imprisoned in Africa, and brought over to America and enslaved. Millions did not make it through the transatlantic voyage. The ones too sick were fed to the sharks. If the load needed to be lightened, precious, innocent human lives were thrown overboard and discarded as expendable cargo. Rape, pillage, and murder were the order of the day.

In America, things went from bad to worse. Lynchings, hangings, burnings, rape, discrimination, segregation, institutionalized racism, the denial of civil rights, Uncle Toms, and bombs were the order of the day. My, my, my! Nearly 400 years of bondage. My country tears to thee, there was no freedom for blacks living in this sweet land of liberty. How sad, a people on whose shoulders this country was built, a people who fought and died for this country in time of war, a people ready to fight for right and against wrong, a people who had to live with no basic human rights in this country that pledges "truth and justice for all." How sad.

Despite the hardships, imprisoned and enslaved African Americans found strength and grace from God to run this race. Yes, God, our heavenly Father, looked down from the height of His sanctuary, from heaven the Lord viewed the earth, to hear the groaning of the prisoner, to loose those appointed to die (cf. Psalm 102:19-20). Yes, God shed his grace on the African American. Yes, God blessed the African American pilgrims as they traveled through this foreign land, this strange land of chains and cords, glass ceilings and fork-tongued, demon-possessed souls. African Americans proved to be strong, spirited, spiritual, clever, and industrious.

Africans quickly learned that the God the Americans claimed to serve was the very same God that delivered the Israelites from Egypt to a land flowing with milk and honey. The Bible says one reason God allowed Egypt to become so mighty was so that, when He delivered the Israelites, His name would be declared in all the earth (Exodus 9:16). Many African slaves already knew this God of Abraham, Isaac, and Jacob before coming to America. There is evidence that Christianity reached West Africa as early as 1402.[3] It wasn't until 1619 that twenty indentured servants arrived in Jamestown, Virginia, from the west coast of Africa. In 1661 the colony of Virginia made Negro slavery legal.[4]

Enslaved Africans knew that, like the children of Israel, God would deliver His black children living in racist America to a new America, a land flowing with the milk and honey of liberty and justice for all. Encouraged with this spiritual insight, black people living in America not only survived, they thrived. By the grace of God through the special gift of the Negro spiritual, the African American worked in the heat of the day, labored hard, and, by the sweat of the brow and ingenuity of the mind, became the backbone that built this great nation. And at the same time African Americans demonstrated to the world how to press on the upward way and wade through the treacherous and often bloody battles for human rights.

African Americans demonstrated the power of prayer when we prayed for the Lord to plant our feet on higher ground as we marched for years with tears from a gloomy past up the stony road called truth and justice for all. African Americans demonstrated the miraculous and mysterious power of the Negro spirituals, which were like oracles from heaven and instruments of God's amazing grace.

It's a highway to heaven, and as African Americans marched we sang songs that not only lifted us up but all people acquainted with grief and sorrow. From slavery to civil rights we sang songs like, "Oh, Freedom (Before I'd Be a Slave)", "Ain't Gonna Let Nobody Turn Me 'Round (Don't Let Nobody Turn You 'Round)", "Paul and Silas (Hold On)" and "This Little Light of Mine."[5] Yes, we demonstrated and illustrated how, against all odds, to keep on marching, to keep on walking, to keep on moving up the king's highway.

STORY

Well, back to the story. While Leo lay on the beach, almost dead, recovering from the vicissitudes, the ups and downs that fate had dealt him, the little people hung ropes, chains, and cords around his neck and other parts of his battered and bruised body. All of a sudden, Leo took a deep breath, yawned, and in a loud voice said, "Yo, Ho, Ho, Ho, Ho." He got up, breaking the ropes they'd tried to tie him down with, as though they were mere strings of thread. Many little people screamed in fear and horror, "He is alive, He is alive," but some rejoiced.

THIRD AND FINAL CALL
(GOD'S MISSIONARY CALL)

The African American church can be referred to as the "sleeping giant." This is because, with a few exceptions, the African American church has not been a significant factor in sending missionaries to the foreign mission field in the latter part of the twentieth century, in violation of God's missionary call.

There are untold reasons why African Americans had practically disappeared from the foreign mission field by the mid 1930s. Some factors were beyond our control. You how it is, light bill due, but you gave the light bill money to sister Jones, who needed to bury her child, who was killed in a church bombing. Phone bill due, but you gave the money to Uncle Bill to bail out his son who was falsely accused of looking at a white woman. By the way, the son never made it to trial, he was lynched. My, my, my! The Ku Klux Klan, at it again.

Even though the African American church has fallen behind in its payments toward God's missionary call, the time to correct this situation has finally come. Good gogglely wogglely ! It took a little while, but that's how long it took for the African American church to gather up what we needed to pay the bill. It took a while for us to gather enough experience of being cast down, rejected, and cast out of mainstream society. It took a while to gather enough experience of being treated as a second-class citizen. It took a while to gather enough experience of being lynched, set afire, and denied basic human rights simply because of the color of our skin. It took a while to gather enough experience to try and prove that the nonviolent civil rights movement was the right path to justice and moral and social change. It took a while to gather the experience of what it meant to be black living in America. But we got what it takes now. In fact we got more than enough in our account to take care of God's business.

The African American is uniquely prepared to fulfill a very special role in God's mission. Many people recognize this, and this is why some missiologists may refer to the African American church as a "sleeping giant." Not only can the African American church be described as a "sleeping giant," but I would say the African American church should also be referred to as "God's battle-ax," God's instrument of war for conquering one of the last remaining citadels of satanic power on this earth, Africa and the Middle East.

The universal African American church has accumulated much wisdom, knowledge, and experience from its rich and royal ancestry. From Nimrod, the world's first great leader, we learned that if we act independently of God, we will mess up, no matter how great we are (Genesis 11:1-9). The Queen of Sheba traveled a great distance to deposit pearls of wisdom in our account (Luke 11:31; cf. 1 Kings 10:1-13). From 400 years under the affliction and yoke of racism we have learned to lean on the everlasting arms of Christ, who endured such hostility from sinners against Himself, lest we become weary and discouraged (cf. Hebrews 12:3). It took time for the lesson of Nimrod's life and the wisdom of Ethiopia to become solidified and enriched by our own experience with slavery and racism. The African American church knows without a doubt that God may not come when we want, but He is always right on time, and when God shows up, God shows out![5]

The experiences of African Americans in America have uniquely prepared and opened doors for the African American church to bring the Gospel message to different people groups around the world. Some of the remaining and more resistant people groups view Anglo-Saxon Americans as representative of arrogant Western imperialism. In many instances this cultural barrier does not exist for the African American.

Skin color matters. It creates and eliminates cultural barriers. Dark-skinned people were regarded to be cursed in this country. But God flipped the switch. God made dark-skinned people in America a blessing to the nations. Often blacks can blend in non-Western cultures better than whites because of skin color. Often whites are tagged with the negative stereotype of Western imperialism. Skin color, this thing in America that simply won't go away, may be the cutting edge of God's battle-ax that will destroy Satan's few remaining strongholds on earth.

Oppression and the fight for basic human rights still exists for people of all colors, and different people groups around the world want to know more about how the African Americans launched and won the fight for civil rights in America. Our answer is, of course, "Leaning on the Lord." Well, how do you lean on the Lord when you are being oppressed and denied basic human rights? Well, have you heard about the power of prayer and what is this thing called the Negro spiritual? "In addition to being the taproot of many musical forms, the Negro spiritual teaches all people how to persevere through adversity."[6]

The retelling of the story of how African Americans won civil rights is not only deeply rooted in the Gospel but it represents our gift to the world and our past-due payment toward God's mission. This illustrates the Gospel message of liberty to those who are oppressed (cf. Luke 4:18-19)! This is our contribution to finishing God's missionary task of not only preaching the Gospel to all peoples of the earth but starting indigenous church movements within their communities. This is our payment for time missed on the mission field.

Most unreached people groups, communities who have never heard the Gospel message, who do not have the Bible translated into their language, who do not have a church in their community, live in North Africa and Asia. This region is sometimes referred to as the10/40 Window, that is, the area between the latitudes 10 degrees and 40 degrees north of the equator and between the Atlantic and Pacific oceans. North Africa accounts for almost half of the 10/40 region. North Africa is our homeland, our backyard. Our kinfolk live there, and they need us. God is calling the African American church to reach people around the world, especially our kinfolk in Africa, and share the Good News of the Gospel and help them develop an indigenous, self-sustaining church movement in their communities.

The African American church has been blessed. The African American church is rich. And now is time for the African American church to pay its debt. Now is the time. It is time for the African American church to wake up and take our rightful place in God's missionary plan. I declare that "Operation Close the Window," the operation led by the African–American church to reach the unreached in the 10/40 Window, is now in effect! Yo, Ho, Ho, Ho, Ho!

CONCLUSION

Surely been 'buked and surely been scorned,
Yo, Ho, Ho, Ho, Ho,
But still my soul is a-heaven born,
Yo, Ho, Ho, Ho, Ho,
If you don't know that I been redeemed,
Yo, Ho, Ho, Ho, Ho,
Just follow me down to Jordan's stream,
(Negro Spiritual: "Free at Last")

Sound off,
one, two
Sound off,
three, four,
Sound off,
one, two, three, four, one, two, THREE FOUR!

Amazing grace! How sweet the sound,
Yo, Ho, Ho, Ho, Ho,
I once was lost, but now I'm found,
Yo, Ho, Ho, Ho, Ho,
'Twas grace that taught my heart to fear,
Yo, Ho, Ho, Ho, Ho,
How precious did that grace appear,
Yo, Ho, Ho, Ho, Ho,
Thro' many dangers, toils and snares,
Yo, Ho, Ho, Ho, Ho,
'Tis grace that bro't me safe thus far,
(Negro Spiritual: "Can I Ride")
Yo, Ho, Ho, Ho, Ho,

Sound off,
one, two
Sound off,
three, four,
Sound off,
one, two, three, four, one, two, THREE FOUR!

Wake up, people, from your sleep,
Yo, Ho, Ho, Ho, Ho,
Spread the news of the Prince of Peace,
Yo, Ho, Ho, Ho, Ho,
Come on soldiers of the cross,
Yo, Ho, Ho, Ho, Ho,
Victory's ours; Satan's lost,

(Leonidas Johnson)

Yo, Ho, Ho, Ho, Ho,
Sound off,
one, two
Sound off,
three, four,
Sound off,
one, two, three, four, one, two, THREE FOUR!

O, Christians, Can't you rise an' tell
Yo, Ho, Ho, Ho, Ho,
The glories of Immanuel, (Negro Spiritual: "Hallelujah")
Yo, Ho, Ho, Ho, Ho,
I really do believe widout a doubt,
Yo, Ho, Ho, Ho, Ho,
Dat de Christian has a right to shout
(Negro Spiritual: "De Ol' Sheep Done Know de Road")
Yo, Ho, Ho, Ho, Ho,

Sound off,
one, two
Sound off,
three, four,
Sound off,
one, two, three, four, one, two, THREE FOUR!

CHARGE

Soldiers, soldiers of the cross,
Yo, Ho, Ho, Ho, Ho,
Fight for Christ, He's our boss,
Yo, Ho, Ho, Ho, Ho,
He bled and died up on the cross,
Yo, Ho, Ho, Ho, Ho,
For you and me, and all the lost!
Yo, Ho, Ho, Ho, Ho,

Sound off,
one, two
Sound off,
three, four,
Sound off,
one, two, three, four, one, two, THREE FOUR!

Left, Left, Left Right Left
Left, Left, Left Right Left
Left, Left, Left Right Left
Left, Left, Left Right Left

Company.............Halt!

SERMON TAG-ON
African American Battle-Axe
by Leonidas A. Johnson

African Americans

1) **Lead:** **Paul and Silas were bound in Jail,**
   Had no money for to pay the bail,
   Group: Keep your eyes on the throne—Hold on!

2) **Lead:** **Paul and Silas did sing and shout,**
   Jail doors opened and they walked out,
   Group: Keep your eyes on the throne—Hold on!

Chorus

All: **Hold on, Hold on,**
Keep your eyes on the throne—Hold on!

3) **Lead:** **We sang hymns and we sang songs,**
   Kept our eyes on the throne,
   Group: Keep your eyes on the throne—Hold on!

4) **Lead:** **We been 'buked and we been scorned,**
   Talked about as sure as you are born,
   Group: Keep your eyes on the throne—Hold on!

5) **Lead:** **We were wronged and we did fight,**
   For dignity and human rights,
   Group: Keep your eyes on the throne—Hold on!

6) **Lead:** **We seen jail and violence too,**
   But the Lord did see us through,
   Group: Keep your eyes on the throne—Hold on!

7)   **Lead:**   **Negro Spirituals, heavenly songs,**
                  Kept our eyes on His throne,
       Group: Keep your eyes on the throne—Hold on!

Ethiopians/Africans

8)   **Lead:**   **Yes we fought at Adwa,**
                  Italians tried to conquer us,
       Group: Keep your eyes on the throne—Hold on!

9)   **Lead:**   **Mussolini tried again,**
                  Bet he'll never try again,
       Group: Keep your eyes on the throne—Hold on!

10)   **Lead:**   **Lion of Judah saved the day,**
                  He has always led the way,
       Group: Keep your eyes on the throne—Hold on!

11)   **Lead:**   **See the Communists come to town,**
                  See us knock them to the ground,
       Group: Keep your eyes on the throne—Hold on!

12)   **Lead:**   **We seen jail and violence too,**
                  But the Lord did see us through,
       Group: Keep your eyes on the throne—Hold on!

All: Ethiopians/Africans and African Americans

13)   **Lead:**   **Now we walk hand in hand,**
                  African and Americans,
       Group: Keep your eyes on the throne—Hold on!

14)   **Lead:**   **We were wronged and now we fight,**
                  For dignity and human rights,
       Group: Keep your eyes on the throne—Hold on!

15)   **Lead:**   **Jesus, Jesus, give insight.**
                       To lead Your children to the Light,
        Group: Keep your eyes on the throne—Hold on!

INVITATION

Someone here may not know Jesus and the pardoning of sins—your sins, my sins. The Bible says, "And as it is appointed for men to die once, but after this the judgment" (Hebrews 9:27). Are you are living in a way that is contrary to God's will? Is your relationship right with God? If you were to die today, are you prepared to stand before God in judgment? The Bible says, "We shall all stand before the judgment seat of Christ" (Romans 14:10). "For we must all appear before the judgment seat of Christ, that each one may receive the things done in the body, according to what he has done, whether good or bad" (2 Corinthians 5:10). The Bible says, "All have sinned and fall short of glory of God" (Romans 3:23). Sin, sin, sin. Sin is an awful thing. I heard Rev. Barbara Rose say this about sin:

> The most devastating and terrible fact in the universe is sin. The cause of all sorrow and the dread of every man lies in this one small word, sin. It has crippled the nature of man. It has destroyed the inner harmony of man's life. It has robbed him of his nobility. It has caused man to be caught in the devil's trap. All mental disorders, all sickness, all destruction, all wars find their original root in sin. It causes madness in the brain and poison in the heart. It is described in the Bible as a fatal disease that demands a radical cure. It is a tornado on the loose. It is a volcano out of control. It is a roaring lion seeking its prey. It is a streak of lightning headed towards the earth. It is quicksand sucking man under. It is a deadly cancer eating its way into the souls of men. It is a cesspool of corruption contaminating every area

of life. But as someone said, "Sin can keep you from the Bible or the Bible can keep you from sin." For ages men were lost in spiritual darkness. By the disease of sin, made to grope, searching, questioning, and seeking some way out. Man needed someone who could lead him out of the mental confusion and moral torture, someone who could unlock the prison doors and redeem him from the devil's prison.[7]

I've said it once and I'll say it again, sin is a terrible thing.

The Bible says, "For the wages of sin is death, but the gift of God is eternal life in Christ Jesus our Lord" (Romans 6:23). "For God so loved the world that He gave His only begotten Son, that whosoever believes in Him should not perish but have everlasting life" (John 3:16). Yes! Jesus is ready, willing and able to save you from the consequences of sin. The Bible says, "that if you confess with your mouth the Lord Jesus and believe in your heart that God has raised Him from the dead, you will be saved" (Romans 10:9). Whatever you need, Jesus is able. The Bible says, "Therefore He is also able to save to the uttermost those who come to God through Him, since He always lives to make intercession for them" (Hebrews 7:25).

I am so glad, Christ died for me,
>   Way back on Mount Calvary;
>   They stretched Him wide and hung Him high,
>   Blood came streamin' down His side.[8]

Would you come and give your life to Christ?
>   My Jesus cried out with a voice,
>   Bowed His head by His own choice
>   There was darkness over the land,
>   When He died for sinful man.[9]

Jesus is the answer. Come!
>He died with a thorn crown they made,
>Death the price for sin He paid;
>The stain of sin, His blood did clean,
>Whiter than ever been seen.[10]

Come to Jesus while you still can.
>And all the world, did fear His doom,
>When they sealed Him in the tomb;
>They laid Him there, and there He stayed,
>In the tomb, no noise was made.[11]

Leo prayed, "Lord, help me! Save me!" Why don't you?
>But very early third day morn,
>He became my strong tower;
>Yes, early, early Sunday morn,
>Jesus rose, with all power![12]

Jesus is listening. Behold, He stands at the door of your heart and knocks. Can't you hear Him? Can't you feel Him? Won't you let Him in? Softly and tenderly Jesus is calling. Calling, "Dear sinner, come home."

>Power, power, power, power,
>All power, power, power!
>Power, power, power, power,
>All power, power, power![13]

Commit your life to Christ, and join His army of missionaries today. He is recruiting now. You can sign up today. It's hard work, and the pay is low, but the benefits are out of this world! In the sixth chapter of Isaiah, God asked an age-old question that still rings loud and clear: "Whom shall I send, And who will go for Us?" (Isaiah 6:8). Will you answer as did Isaiah, "Here am I! Send me"? (Isaiah 6:8). Answer today! Don't delay! "Behold, now is the accepted time; behold, now is the day of salvation" (2 Corinthians 6:2).

We have done as the Lord has commanded; yet there is still room.

> There's room at the cross for you,
> There's room at the cross for me.
> Though millions have come,
> There's still room for one.
> There is room at the cross for you.

Come…Nobody is in a hurry but the devil…

Our time is far spent. "Thanks be to God, who gives us the victory through our Lord Jesus Christ" (1 Corinthians 15:57).

Amen.

And Amen!

In the sixth chapter of Isaiah, God asked an age-old question that still rings loud and clear: "Whom shall I send, and who will go for Us?" (Isaiah 6:8).

CHAPTER SEVEN

African American Mission Resources

…seek, and you will find;…. (Matthew 7:7 NKJV)

THE FOLLOWING RESOURCES ARE OFFERED IN THE hope that they might prove helpful to churches and individuals interested in exploring how to repsond to God's missionary and having a greater impact on global missions.

ACMC (Advancing Churches in Missions Commitment)

James Kildore, President
4201 N. Peachtree Road #300
Atlanta, GA 30341
(800) 747-7346
atlanta@acmc.org / www.acmc.org

Action International Ministries
Doug Nichols, International Director
P. O. Box 398
Mount Terrace, WA 98043
(425) 775-4800
info@actionintl.org / www.actionintl.org

African Christian Fellowship
(410) 536-5371

African American Center for World Mission
General Director: Rev. Ivor Duberry
Director of Operations: Porcya Duberry
1605 Elizabeth St.
Pasadena, CA 91104
(626) 398-2205
www.aacwm.org / info@www.aacwm.org

African Christian Fellowship
Joseph Richardson
jorichardson@na.cokecce

African American Cultural Center–ETHIOPIA! Project
See The Crystal Fountain Culture and
Vision Center of Reconciliation (CFCAVCOR)

African Methodist Episcopal Church (AME)
Dr. Clement W. Fugh, B.B.A.
General Secretary and Chief Information Officer
500 8th Ave South, Nashville, TN 37203
Phone: (615) 254-0911
Fax: (615) 254-0912
cio@ame-church.com

African Methodist Episcopal Zion Church
Rev. K. J. Degraffenreidt, Secretary/Treasurer
(212) 870-2952
Domkd5@aol.com

Agape Global Missions, Inc
Founder/President: Linda F. Marcell, Ph.D.
815 N. La Brea Avenue, #465
Inglewood, CA 90302
(310) 671-7895
agapegm@yahoo.com

Ambassadors Fellowship
Director: Virgil Amos
(719) 495-8180
102466.2243@compuserve.com

Carver Bible College
Atlanta, Georgia
President: Robert Crummie
(404) 527-4520

Carver International Missions
Director: Glen Mason
(770) 323-0772
carverfm@aol.com

Christian Mission for the Deaf
Berta Foster, Administrator
P.O. Box 28005
Detroit, MI 48228
Phone/TTY/Fax (313) 933-1424
cmd@cmdeaf.org / www.cmdeaf.org

COMINAD
(Cooperative Mission Network of the African Dispersion)
Director: Brian Johnson
P. O. Box 9756
Chesapeake, VA 23321

P. O. Box 6368
Norfolk, VA 23508
(757) 467-5803 / 467-0601
iaamm@aol.com

Christians in Action
President: Elgin Taylor
(559) 564-3762
cinamissions@christiansinaction.org
www.christiansinaction.org

CFCAVCOR
Crystal Fountain Culture
and Vision Center of Reconciliation
d/b/a The African American Cultural
Center—ETHIOPIA! Project
President: Rev. Dr. Leonidas A. Johnson
P. O. Box 4434
Diamond Bar, CA 91765
(909) 396-1201
revleonidas@crystalfountain.org / www.crystalfountain.org

Crystal Fountain Ministries, Inc.
President: Rev. Dr. Leonidas A. Johnson
P.O. Box 4434
Diamond Bar, CA 91765
(909) 396-1201
crystalfountainministries@hotmail.com
www.crystalfountain.org

Friends of Africa Missions Ministries, Inc.
Minister Curtis Barber
1914 Southridge Drive
Edgewood, MD 21040
Tel: (410) 679-1215
barbers19@aol.com

Global Health Outreach
Director: Dr. Sam Moline
P.O. Bx 7500
Bristol, TN 37621-7500
Phone: (888) 230-2637
Fax: (423) 844-1005
www.cmda.org/go/gho

Good News Jail and Prison Ministry
Director: Calvin Scott
(301) 292-4952
hq@gnjpm.org

Great Commission Global Ministries
President: Bishop David Perrin
(301) 316-4132
(800) 707-3521
bishop@gcgm.org / www.gcgm.org

Have Christ Will Travel Ministries
Dr. Joseph C. Jeter, President
528 Church Lane
Philadelphia, PA 19144
(215) 438-6308

Impact International

A Ministry of Campus Crusade for Christ
Contact: Vaughn Walston
 (407) 826-2542
(888) 672-2896
www.impactmovement.com

International Mission Board of the Southern Baptist Convention
African American Church Relations

Contact: David Cornelius
(804) 794-8015
dcornelius@imb.org / www.imb.org

Justice for All/PF Fellowship Ethiopia

President: Rev. Daniel Gebreselassie
P.O. Box 2366 code 1110
Addis Ababa, Ethiopia
gselasie@yahoo.com

Lutheran Church–Missouri Synod Board for Mission Services

Executive Director: Dr. Philip Campbell
(314) 965-9000
(800) 248-1930 ext. 1755
Blackministry@lcms.org
Phillip.campbell@lcms.org

Lott Carey Baptist Mission Convention

Executive Director: Dr. David Goatley
(202) 667-8493
LottCarey@aol.com
www.lottcarey.org

National Baptist Convention of America
President Stephen J. Thurston
www.nbcamerica.net/

National Baptist Convention, USA, Inc.
President: William Shaw
(615) 228-6292
Contact: Elaine Siryon
Berrian2sir@netscape.net
(215) 843-1949
www.nationalbaptist.com

Foreign Mission Board
National Baptist Convention, USA, Inc.
701 South 19th Street
Philadelphia, PA 19146
(215) 735-7868

Navigators—African American Ministries
Contact: Eugene Burrell, Urban & Collegiate Ministries
(719) 598-1212
Home.navigators.org/us/African American/index.cfm

Pan African Christian Exchange
Contact: Gregory Alexander
(248) 557-2499
Galexander1@msn.com

Reconciliation Ministry Network
Contact: Jim Sutherland, Ph.D.
(423) 822-1091
Jim@rmni.org / www.rmni.org

SIM USA—African American Relations
Contact: Ron Sonius
(803) 980-4713
www.sim.org

TEAM—African American Church Mobilization
team@teamworld.org
(630) 653-5300
www.teamworld.org

WEC International, USA
P.O. Box 1707
Fort Washington, PA 19034
(888) 646-6202 / (215) 646-2322
mobilization@wec-usa.org /www.wec-usa.org

World Gospel Mission
3783 State Road, 1-B East
P.O. Box 948
Marion, IN 46952
(765) 664-7331
www.wgm.org

Wycliffe African American Relations
Contact: Gertude Nicholas
(407) 852-3600 / (407) 852-4113
Gertrude_Nicholas@wycliffe.org
www.wycliffe.org

Youth with a Mission—African American Relations
Contact: Orchidy Boyd
(501) 248-7033
Orchi41@yahoo.com

ADDITIONAL MISSION RESOURCES

_____

_____

_____

_____

_____

_____

_____

_____

_____

_____

_____

_____

_____

_____

_____

_____

_____

_____

_____

_____

_____

Holistic Missions: addressing the entire range of human needs of the whole person: the spirit, soul and body.

CHAPTER EIGHT

Glossary of Terms

Those who sow in tears Shall reap in joy. (Psalm 126:5 NKJV)

10/40 Window—The area between the latitudes 10° and 40° north of the equator and between the Atlantic and Pacific oceans. It covers North Africa, Middle East and Asia. The window has most of the world's least-reached peoples and most of the governments that oppose Christianity.

African American Church—African American Christians who are members of a local and/or the universal church. Metaphorically referred to as the "Sleeping Giant," the "Black Giant" and "God's Battle-axe."

African American Cultural Center—*ETHIOPIA!* Project — Also known as Operation Close the Window. The official name of the organization is The Crystal Fountain Culture and Vision Center of Reconciliation (CFCAVCOR).

Absolute Poverty—Describes situations in which people have an absolute insufficiency to meet their basic needs.

Ante-Diluvian(s), also Pre-diluvian(s)—Meaning before the Deluge and referring to those who lived before the Flood described in Genesis 6—8.

Battle-axe—a mallet or heavy war-club. Applied metaphorically (Jeremiah 51:20) to Cyrus, God's instrument in destroying Babylon. Dr. Leonidas A. Johnson applies "God's Battle-axe" metaphorically to the African American Church, God's instrument in God's Mission.

Black Giant—Applied metaphorically by Leonidas A. Johnson to the African American church in God's mission.

Church Planting Movement—Continuing to reproduce fellowships capable of evangelizing the rest of its people group.

Community Development—Aims to enable local people to mobilize local resources to meet basic needs in an enduring way throughout an entire community.

Contextualization—To present something with regard to the cultural context. Adapting ourselves and our presentation of God's message to the culture of the receiving people.

Culture—The integrated systems of beliefs, feelings, values and their associated symbols, and patterns of behavior and products shared by a group of people.

E-Scale—Helps compare the cultural distances that Christians need to move in order to communicate the gospel with others. E0 refers to renewal evangelism of church-going Christians. E1 refers to evangelism of non-Christians with no contact with the church. E2 refers to evangelism of non-Christians in a similar but different culture. E3 refers to evangelism of non-Christians in a completely different culture.

Ethiopia—one of the oldest Christian civilizations in the world, has the longest archeological record of any country on earth, and is also credited with being the original home of humanity.

Ethnocentrism—Based on our natural tendency to judge the behavior of people in other cultures by the values and assumptions of our own.

Evangelism—When a church movement seeks to reach others of their own culture with the Gospel of Jesus Christ.

Foreign mission—global/cross-cultural mission ministry.

Frontier Missions—Cross-cultural work that seeks to establish a Christian people movement within people groups where it does not yet exist.

Global—Pertaining to or involving the entire earth; worldwide.

God's Battle-axe—Applied metaphorically to the African American Church, God's instrument in God's Mission, by Leonidas A. Johnson.

God's Mission—also *missio Dei*. God's pronouncement to redeem humans back to Himself from every people group of the world. God's will to redeem humans back to Himself from every people group of the world. Note: God's divine purpose and goal is threefold. First, God's goal is to reveal Himself that His name would be glorified. Secondly, God's goal is to destroy satan, sin and death. Thirdly, God's goal is to establish His kingdom by redeeming and reconciling unto Himself true worshipers from every people group. This third goal reveals that God is on a mission to save humanity that we may freely worship Him. This third goal incorporates the first and second goals.

Goers—Cross-cultural workers in the field who seek to take the Gospel to the lost.

Gospelizer—are God-sent messengers whose holistic witness brings the Good News of Christ's presence and redeeming mission to humanity.

Ham— indicating "hot," "heat," "black." Second son of Noah. The father of Black/African peoples.

Holistic Missions—Seeks to address the entire range of human needs of the whole person: the spirit, soul and body. This includes material, social, as well as community economics, social and political.

Home mission—local/urban mission ministry.

Indigenous—Not seen as foreign.

Justice for All.../PF Fellowship—A Nongovernmental Organization (NGO) in Ethiopia whose primary focus is to change the living conditions of prisoners, ex-prisoners, victims and prisoners' families in Ethiopia. It works closely with the criminal justice system and the community. It also works closely with CFCAVCOR and is a sponsor/partner of the African American Cultural Center—*ETHIOPIA!* project.

Kebra Negast—Queen of Sheba legend.

Local Church—*ekklesia* in its primary and literal sense—a visible, local congregation of Christian disciples, meeting for worship, instruction and service.

Missionary—A Christian missionary is one commissioned by a local church to evangelize, plant churches and disciple people away from their home area and often among people of a different race, culture or language.

Mobilizers—Those who channel key resources, training and vision for world evangelism to the Body of Christ.

Nations—The Greek is *ethne* or *ethnos*, which is translated "ethnic groups."

Non-Western World—The countries of Latin America, Africa and Asia.

Nimrod—Descendant of Ham. The sixth son of Cush. One of our great Black ancestors.

Nominal Christians—Being such in name only.

Operation Close the Window—Term used by Leonidas Johnson to refer to the function of the African–American Church as an instrument of God to reach the unreached in the 10/40 Window, namely Africa, the Mid East and Asia, facilitated by the African American Cultural Center —*ETHIOPIA!* project.

P-Scale—Helps compare the different cultural distances that potential converts need to move in order to join the nearest church. P0 refers to a people participating in a local culturally relevant church. P1 refers to a people whose culture contains a local church. P2 refers to a people without a church whose culture is similar to a people with a church. P3 refers to a people without a church whose culture is very different from that of the nearest group with a church.

People Movement—A movement of a large number of non-Christians in a particular people group into the Church.

People group—A significantly large sociological grouping of individuals who perceive themselves to have a common affinity with one another because of their shared language, religion, ethnicity, residence, occupation, class or caste, situation, etc., or combination of these. From the viewpoint of evangelization, this is the largest possible group within which the gospel can be spread without encountering barriers of understanding or acceptance.

Political Liberation—Focuses on oppressive regimes, violation of human rights.

Reached Peoples—Describes those peoples who have a strong Christian Movement among them and are able to go and evangelize their own people.

Relative Poverty—Describes situations in which people are on the margins of society. A person's standard of living is compared in relation to others in the community or nation.

Relief—Aims at providing basic necessities for survival for victims of war, natural disasters and prolonged injustice.

Senders—Believers on the home front with a world vision, who actively support the "goers."

Sleeping Giant—Applied metaphorically to the African American Church.

Unchurched People—People who don't go to church but who have strong Christian churches that they could attend if they desired.

Universal Church—*ekklesia* in its secondary and figurative sense—the invisible, universal company, including all of God's true people on earth and in heaven.

Unreached Peoples—Ethno-linguistic group within which there is no indigenous community of believing Christians able to evangelize this people group. It should be a measure of the exposure of a people group to the gospel and not a measure of the response.

Queen of Sheba—African Queen identified with Ethiopia. She visited King Solomon according to the Bible (2 Chronicles 9:1-12).

Queen of Sheba Legend—Visited King Solomon and had a son by Solomon named Menilek. Menilek later traveled to Jerusalem to see his father, brought back the Ark of the Covenant and founded a dynasty of kings which reigned in Ethiopia for close to three thousand years. Explained in a book called *Kebra Negast*.

Viable—Growing on its own.

Welcomers—Those who reach out to internationals in their own country.

Western World—The countries of Europe, North America, and Australasia.

Worldview—A people group's mental map of their world. Their worldview is made up of their beliefs, feelings, values and how they relate to the rest of the world.

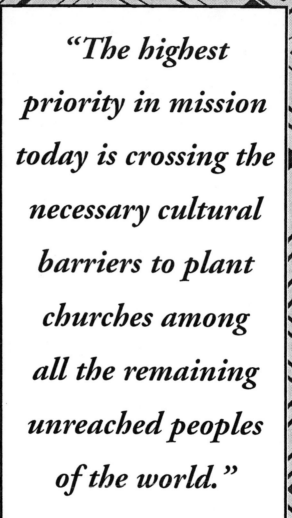

"The highest priority in mission today is crossing the necessary cultural barriers to plant churches among all the remaining unreached peoples of the world."

(U.S. Center for World Mission)

APPENDIX

Strategy

Now all things are of God, who has reconciled us to Himself through Jesus Christ, and has given us the ministry of reconciliation,.... (2 Corinthians 5:18, NKJV)

CFCAVCOR

The Crystal Fountain Culture and Vision Center of Reconciliation

I. Why should African Americans be concerned about Africa?

    A. Africa is our Motherland. Africans and African Americans are part of the same family.

    B. Africa needs us.

        1. Africans need our help obtaining modern resources and technology.

        2. Principle: "God blesses us to be blessings to others."

C. We need them.
   1. Africa provides the missing link to our African American heritage.
   2. One-sided TV and Western depictions of Africa: Poor, remote, tribal, disease, drought, famine; jungle, animals.
D. God is concerned about Africa: Northern Africa and Arabia is home to about half of all unreached people groups in the world (i.e. people of different cultures that have never heard the Gospel message nor God's plan of salvation through Christ.

II. Why build an African American Cultural Center in Africa?

   A. It will serve as a tool to mobilize African American missionaries.
      1. It will serve as a Jerusalem, a religious Mecca for the army of African American missionaries God has established for a time such as this.
      2. "The highest priority in mission today is crossing the necessary cultural barriers to plant churches among all the remaining unreached peoples of the world" (U.S. Center for World Mission).
   B. Secondary benefits:
      1. It will serve as a cultural Mecca for Africans, African Americans and all peoples of African descent in the Diaspora.
      2. It will serve as commercial Mecca for travelers, business people and the international business community.
      3. It will serve as an international reconciliatory and human rights center for the peoples of the world.

III. Why Ethiopia? What Makes Ethiopia so Special?

   A. Because of what is said about Ethiopia by Greek historians, world leaders, God (Ethiopia mentioned more than 39 times in KJV Bible, e.g., Amos 9:7; Psalm 68:31).

   B. Because of what is in Ethiopia.

      1. Christian heritage.

         a. Kebra Nagast: Queen of Sheba and King Solomon; Solomonic kings.

         b. Religious artifacts: notably, per legend, Ark of Covenant.

      2. Eight attractions declared World Heritage Treasures by UNESCO, including Axum, Lalibela, Gonder, Bahar Dar.

      3. Sociopolitical factors: center for African leaders; African Unity (AU); uninterrupted history—only African country never colonized; ancestral kinship with Arabia; respect from Islamic, Jewish, and Christian communities.

   C. Because of what comes from Ethiopia.

      1. Cradle of humanity—Garden of Eden.

      2. The answer to the African American experience and heritage.

IV. Will African Americans travel to Africa?

   A. YES! African Americans will travel to Africa.

      1. Many African Americans have a natural curiosity about Africa and a deep desire to make a spiritual and/or cultural pilgrimage to their ancestral home.

      2. Many African Americans want to help the poor Africans they see on TV.

V. Why now?

    A. We have entered into the age of end-time ministry.

        1. Approaching the completion of the "Great Mission," According to Dr. Ralph Winter, "The opportunity before us is not to evangelize six billion one by one, but to start an indigenous church movement within an estimated 10,000 unreached groups which are yet to be discipled."

        2. "And this gospel of the kingdom will be preached in all the world as a witness to all the nations, and then the end will come" (Matt. 24:14).

    B. God is opening doors of opportunity.

    C. God is looking for the return on His investment.

        1. What He has invested in African Americans. Remember the thousands who suffered and died in our struggle for freedom and basic human rights.

        2. What He has invested in Ethiopia. Thousands of Ethiopians suffered and died to preserve their independence and Christian heritage (Matt. 12:42).

    D. Millennium celebration in Ethiopia: 2007. Will attempt to have ministry partially operational by this time.

VI. Where are we now?

    A. Incorporation of The Crystal Fountain Culture and Vision Center of Reconciliation (CFCAVCOR) as nonprofit 501(c)(3), April 15, 2004.

    B. Partnership established with sponsoring organization in Ethiopia—Justice for All/PF Ethiopia.

    C. Meeting and approval to proceed from Minister of Culture, Ethiopia.

    D. Pledge of support from Consulate General, Ethiopia.

VII. What next?

A. Pray: "Let Your work appear to Your servants And Your glory to their children. And let the beauty of the Lord our God be upon us, And establish the work of our hands for us; Yes, establish the work of our hands" (Ps. 90:16-17 NKJV).

   1. Will go the humanitarian route: criticism and fire from both religious and nonreligious communities.

   2. The Lord our God is the Man with the Master Plan: I move at His command.

B. Share the plan with colleagues.

   1. Recruit Advisory/Steering Committee members

   2. Seek referrals and recommendations to funding sources and potential donors

C. Start establishing local chapters to aid in national mobilization effort.

OPEN NOW THE CRYSTAL FOUNTAIN

1. Guide me, O Thou
       great Jehovah,
   Pilgrim thro' this
       barren land;
   I am weak but,
       Thou art mighty,
   Hold me with Thy
       powerful hand:
   Bread of Heaven,
       feed me till I want no more;
   Bread of Heaven,
       feed me till I want no more.

2. Open now the
       crystal fountain
   Whence the healing
       waters flow;
   Let the fiery
       cloudly pillar
   Lead me all my
       journey through:
   Strong Deliverer,
       be Thou still my Strength and Shield;
   Strong Deliverer,
       be Thou still my Strength and Shield.

3. When I tread
        the verge of Jordan,
   Bid my anxious
        fears subside;
   Bear me through
        the swelling current,
   Land me safe
        on Canaan's side:
   Songs of praises,
        I will ever give to Thee;
   Songs of praises,
        I will ever give to Thee.

   (William Williams)

4. And when I come,
        to Canaan's band;
   And must fight to,
        claim the land.
   Strength and wisdom
        give to me;
   Grace and favor,
        victory.
   God's on mission,
        every tribe shall worship Thee!
   God's on mission,
        every tribe shall worship Thee!

   (Leonidas A. Johnson)

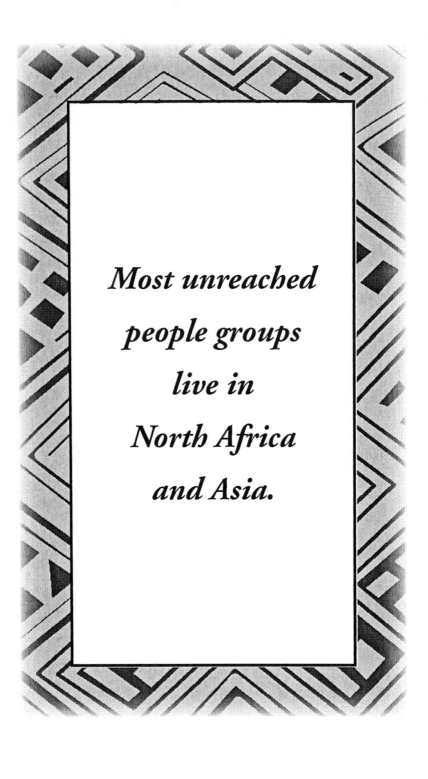

*Most unreached
people groups
live in
North Africa
and Asia.*

BIBLIOGRAPHY

"...you shall receive power when the Holy Spirit has come upon you; and you shall be witnesses to Me in Jerusalem, and in all Judea and Samaria, and to the end of the earth." (Acts 1::8, NKJV)

Ayele, Negussay. *Ethiopia and the United States Volume One: The Season of Courtship, United States: Ocopy.com, 2003.*

Blincoe, Robert. *The Golden Thread Through Scripture.* Pasadena, Calif.: Frontiers, 2001.

Bosch, David. *Transforming Mission: Paradigm Shifts in Theology of Mission.* Maryknoll, NY: Orbis Books, 1991.

Brooks, Miguel F., compiler, ed., trans. *Kebra Negast (The Glory of Kings): The True Ark of the Covenant.* Lawrenceville: The Red Sea Press, Inc., 2000.

Hawthorne, Steven. *Perspectives on the World Christian Movement Study Guide, 1999 ed.* Pasadena: William Carey Library, 1999.

Isaac, Ephraim. "Is the Ark of the Covenant in Ethiopia?" *Biblical Archaeology Review* July/August 1993.

Jenkins, Philip. *The Next Christendom: The Coming of Global Christianity.* New York: Oxford University Press, 2002.

Johnson, Leonidas. *Bread of Heaven: Devotional Guide Featuring Old Meter Hymns, 2nd ed.* Diamond Bar: Crystal Fountain Publications, 2000.

Johnson, Leonidas. *Go Down Moses! Daily Devotions Inspired by Old Negro Spirituals,* Valley Forge: Judson Press, 2000.

Johnson, Leonidas. *Midnight Love Devotional: Love, Sex, Holiness Song of Solomon's Secret.* Diamond Bar: Crystal Fountain Publications, 2005.

Johnson, Leonidas. *The Foolishness of the Message Preached: An Original Collection of Soul Food-Filled Sermons, Vol. One.* Diamond Bar: Crystal Fountain Publications, 1999.

Johnson, Leonidas. *The Foolishness of the Message Preached: An Original Collection of Soul Food-Filled Sermons, Vol. Two.* Diamond Bar: Crystal Fountain Publications, 2000.

Johnson, Leonidas. *Solomon's Prayer: Heal the Land: Devotional Readings from the King.* Diamond Bar: Crystal Fountain Publications, 2002.

McCray, Walter A. *Gospelizers Terrorized and Intensified.* Chicago: Black Light Fellowship, 2002.

McCray, Walter A. *The Black Presence in the Bible: Discovering the Black and African Identity of Biblical Persons and Nations, Vol. 1.* Chicago: Black Light Fellowship, 1990.

McKissic, Sr., William Dwight. *Beyond Roots: In Search of Blacks in the Bible.* Renaissance Productions Inc.: New Jersey, 1990.

Merahi, Kessis Kefyalew. *The Contribution of the Orthodox Tewahedo Church To the Ethiopian Civilization.* Addis Ababa: Kessis Merahi, 1999.

Pankhurst, Richard. *The Ethiopians: A History.* Oxford: Blackwell Publishers, 2001.

Patrick, John. *The Progress of the Afro-American.* Westchester Illinois: Benefic Press, 1969.

Sanneh, Lamin. *West African Christianity: The Religious Impact.* London: C. Hurst and Co., 1983.

Sawyer, David. *Work of the Church: Getting the Job Done in Boards and Committees.* Judson Press: Valley Forge, 2001.

Sutherland, Jim. RMNI, Reconciliation Ministries Network. <www.rni.org>.

Walston, Vaughn J. and Robert J. Stevens, eds. *African American Experience in World Mission: A Call Beyond Community.* Pasadena: William Carey Library, 2002.

Winter, Ralph and Steven Hawthorne, eds. *Perspectives on the World Christian Movement: A Reader, Third Edition.* Pasadena: William Carey Library, 1999.

Winter, Ralph, ed. *Mission Frontiers: Special Issue: "The African American and Missions: the Past; the Present; the Possibilities."* U.S. Center for World Mission 2002.

Wesley, Charles H. *International Library of Negro Life and History: In Freedom's Footsteps from the African Background to the Civil War.* New York: Publishers Company Inc., 1969

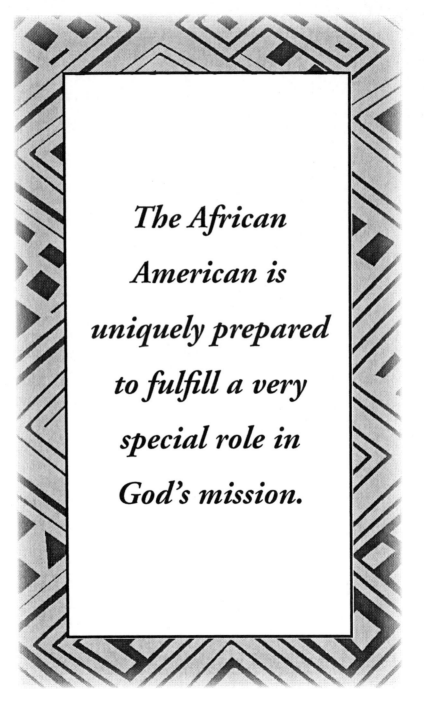

The African American is uniquely prepared to fulfill a very special role in God's mission.

"What hinders me from being baptized?" (Acts 8:36, NKJV)

CHAPTER ONE

1. Lynn Marcell is a missionary and is president of Agape Global Missions. She co-chaired an educational task force of the African American Center for World Mission in Pasadena, Calif.

2. Esker J. Harris is an African American missionary to Malawi sent from the National Baptist Convention, USA, Inc., and is currently on education sabbatical at Fuller Seminary, Pasadena, working on his doctorate. He also served on the educational task force of the African American Center for World Mission.

3. Leonidas Johnson, "The Red Yellow Brick Road." In *The Foolishness of the Message Preached: An Original Collection*

of Soul Food Filled Sermons, Vol. 2 (Diamond Bar, Calif.: Crystal Fountain Publications, 2000), 155-168.

4. Ibid., 168.

5. Robert Blincoe, *The Golden Thread Through Scripture: Biblical Proofs of God's Plan that the Blessings which Came to Abraham Should Also Come to the Ethne* (Pasadena, Calif.: Frontiers, 2001).

6. Walter A. McCray, *Gospelizers Terrorized and Intensified* (Chicago: Black Light Fellowship, 2002), 40.

7. Ibid., 40-41.

8. Walter C. Kaiser, Jr., "Israel's Missionary Call." In *Perspectives on the World Christian Movement, Third Edition*, ed. Ralph D. Winter and Steven C. Hawthorne (Pasadena: William Carey Library, 1999), 10-16.

9. Patrick Johnstone, "The Church Is Bigger Than You Think." In *Perspectives on the World Christian Movement, A Reader, Third Edition*, ed. by Ralph D. Winter and Steven C. Hawthorne (Pasadena: William Carey Library, 1999), 217.

10. Ibid., 217.

11. Steven Hawthorne, ed., *Perspectives on the World Christian Movement Study Guide* (Pasadena: William Carey Library, 1999), 48.

12. Richard Pankhurst, *The Ethiopians: A History* (Massachusetts: Blackwell Publishers, copyright 2001), 34.

13. Lamin Sanneh, *West African Christianity: The Religious Impact* (London: C. Hurst and Co., 1983), 15-34.

14. Ralph Winter and Steve Hawthorne, "The Kingdom Strikes Back." In *Perspectives on the World Christian Movement, Third Ed.*, 195-196.

15. Ibid., 196-197.

16. Ibid., 199.

17. Ibid., 206.

18. Nancy Shute, "Where We Come From: Recent advances in genetics are starting to illuminate the wanderings of early humans." *U.S. News & World Report* January 29, 2001: 36-41.

19. Pankhurst, 1.

20. Kessis Kefyalew Merahi, *The Contribution of the Orthodox Tewahedo Church to the Ethiopian Civilization* (Addis Ababa: Kessis Merahi, 1999), 34-38.

21. William McKissic, *Beyond Roots: In Search of Blacks in the Bible* (New Jersey: Renaissance Productions Inc., 1990), 16.

22. Ibid., 34.

23. Walter A. McCray, *The Black Presence in the Bible: Discovering the Black and African Identity of Biblical Persons and Nations* (Chicago: Black Light Fellowship 1990), 61.

24. McKissic, 32.

25. McCray (1990), 69-70.

26. According to Esker Harris, East Africa was very desirable for Europeans. The high mountainous areas of Kenya, Uganda, etc., were too high for mosquitoes to thrive, so malaria was not so great a threat. White agencies reserved East Africa mostly for themselves and sent blacks to mosquito-infested West Africa.

27. Harris notes that Emma B. Delaney and Rev. Landon Cheek, two National Baptist missionaries, helped establish the Providence Industrial Mission in Malawi. Delaney also served in Liberia and opened a new mission station there.

28. Marylin Lewis, "Overcoming Obstacles: The Broad Sweep of the African American and Missions. *Mission Frontiers Special Issue, The African American and Missions: the Past; the Present; the Possibilities*, 2002.

29. David Cornelius, "A Brief Historical Survey of African American Involvement in International Missions." In

African American Experience in World Mission: A Call Beyond Community, ed. Vaugh Walston and Robert Stevens, 48.

30. McCray (1990), 78.

31. Ibid., 153-154. See also footnotes in McCray.

32. Vaughn J. Walston and Robert J. Stevens, *African American Experience in World Mission: A Call Beyond Community* (Pasadena: William Carey Library, 2002).

33. Jim Sutherland, *Reconciliation Ministries Network.* <http://www.rmni.org>.

34. Negussay Ayele, *Ethiopia and the United States: Volume I, the Season of Courtship,* 24-28.

35. Ralph Winter and Bruce A. Koch, "Finishing the Task." In *Perspectives, Third Ed.,* 509-524.

36. Ibid.

37. Ibid.

38. Ralph Winter, "The Task Can Be Completed," USCWM brochure.

39. Patrick Johnstone, "Covering the Globe." In *Perspectives, Third Ed.,* 541-552.

40. Leonidas Johnson, "Approaching God in an Age of Adversity." In *Solomon's Prayer: Devotions from the King* (Diamond Bar: Crystal Fountain Publications, 2002), 59-75.

41. Leonidas Johnson, "Have You Considered Ethiopia?" In *Midnight Love Devotional: Love, Sex, Holiness—Song of Solomon's Secret* (Diamond Bar: Crystal Fountain Publications, 2005), 85-117.

42. Leonidas Johnson, *Bread of Heaven: Songs of Praise Daily Biblical Devotional Guide Featuring Old Meter Hymns* (Diamond Bar: Crystal Fountain Publications, 2000), 99.

43. Miguel F. Brooks, compiler, editor and translator, *Kebra Negast (The Glory of Kings): The True Ark of the Covenant* (Lawrenceville: The Red Sea Press, 2000), 33, 42, 45, 62, 81.

44. Ephraim Isaac, "Is the Ark of the Covenant in Ethiopia?" *Biblical Archeology Review* (July/August 1993): 60-63.

45. Pankhurst, 20.

46. Justice for All/PF Fellowship was formerly known as Prison Fellowship Ethiopia (PFE), an established and well-respected Ethiopian NGO (non-governmental organization). The new name is a reflection of PFE's success and testimony to its great impact both inside and outside the prison system.

CHAPTER TWO

1. Leonidas Johnson, *The Foolishness of the Message Preached,* 139-154.

2. Philip Jenkins, *The Next Christendom: The Coming of Global Christianity* (New York: Oxford Press, 2002), 1.

3. Ibid., 2

4. Ibid., 3

5. Ibid.

6. Ibid., 12.

7. Ibid., 13

8. Ibid.,15

9. Ibid., 16.

10. Ibid., 17.

11. Negussay Ayele, *Ethiopia and the United States: The Season of Courtship*, 39.

12. Jenkins, 18.

13. Ibid., 19.

14. Isaac, 61.

15. Ayele, 35.

16. Jenkins, 19

17. Leonidas Johnson, *Go Down Moses.*

CHAPTER THREE

1. Symposium survey, African American Center for World Mission.

CHAPTER FOUR

1. Kwesi Kamau, "Missions: A Christ-Centered Worldview. " The 40th Celebration of the National Black Evangelical Association, June 2-5 2004, Los Angeles, Calif.

2. *Mission Frontiers Special Issue*, 21

3. Jenkins, 93.

4 Ibid., 93-94.

5. National Coordinator, P.O. Box 368, Norfolk, VA 23508. <IAAMM@aol.com>.

CHAPTER FIVE

1. David Sawyer, *The Work of the Church: Getting the Job Done in Boards and Committees* (Valley Forge: Judson Press, 2001), 31.

2. David Bosch, *Transforming Mission: Paradigm Shifts in Theology of Mission* (Maryknoll, NY: Orbis Books), 390.

3. Ivor Duberry, "Mountain View Community Church Missions Program Proposal 2004-2005," Mountain View Community Church, Temecula, Calif., John Wells, Senior Pastor.

4. Jim Sutherland, Director, Reconciliation Ministry Network. <http:\\www.rmni.org>.

CHAPTER SIX

1. Charles H. Wesley, *International Library of Negro Life and History: In Freedom's Footsteps—From the African Background to the Civil War* (New York: Publishers Company, Inc., 1969), 39.

2. Leonidas Johnson, *Bread of Heaven Songs of Praise 2nd ed.: Daily Biblical Devotional Guide Featuring Old Meter Hymns* (Diamond Bar: Crystal Fountain Publications, 2000), 99.

3. Lamin Sanneh, *West African Christianity: The Religious Impact* (London: C. Hurst and Co., 1983), 19.

4. John Patrick, *The Progress of the Afro-American* (Westchester, Ill.: Benefic Press, 1969), 33.

5. Leonidas Johnson, *Go Down Moses! Daily Devotions Inspired by Old Negro Spirituals* (Valley Forge: Judson Press, 2000), ix.

6. Leonidas Johnson, *Solomon's Prayer—Heal the Land: Devotional Readings from the King*, (Diamond Bar: Crystal Fountain Publications, 2002), 63.

7. Compiled from African American preaching tradition.

8. Johnson, Leonidas, *The Foolishness of the Message Preached*, 176.

9. Ibid.

10. Ibid.

11. Ibid.

12. Ibid.

13. Ibid.

*Africa is one of
the last remaining
frontiers in God's
missionary plan to
gather a remnant
within each
of the world's
people groups.*

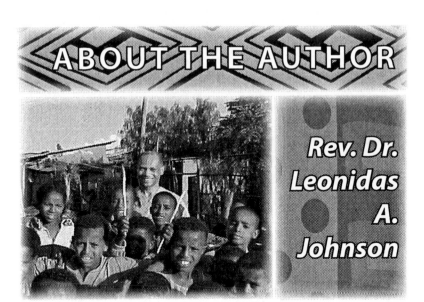

Rev. Dr. Leonidas A. Johnson

Go therefore and make disciples of all nations, baptizing them in the name of the Father and of the Son and of the Holy Spirit. (Matthew 28:19, NKJV)

THE REVEREND DR. LEONIDAS A. JOHNSON IS a licensed optometrist and third-generation preacher. He has authored several books and made several missionary trips to Africa.

Dr. Johnson is the founder of Crystal Fountain Ministries, Inc., a 501(c)(3) nonprofit religious corporation and The Crystal Fountain Culture and Vision Center of Reconciliation, a 501 (c)(3) nonprofit public benefit organization designed to facilitate the establishment and implementation of the African American Culture Center—*ETHIOPIA!* project. He also served as co-chair of the Education Task Force of the African American Center for World Mission, Pasadena, California and was a contributing editor of their Beyond Community Workshop Handbook.

Dr. Johnson was awarded a Bachelor of Arts degree from Illinois Wesleyan University, in Bloomington, Illinois, and a Bachelor of Science degree and a Doctor of Optometry degree from the Southern California College of Optometry, Fullerton, California. He also earned a Master of Arts degree from Talbot School of Theology, Biola University, La Mirada, California.

Date *February 27, 2006*

No. *045/CA/06*

የኢትዮጵያ ቆንስላ ጄኔራል ጽ/ቤት
ሎስ አንጀለስ
CONSULATE GENERAL OF ETHIOPIA
LOS ANGELES

Rev. Dr. Leonidas A. Johnson
President
The Crystal Fountain Culture
and Vision Center of Reconciliation (CFCAVCOR)

Dear Rev. Dr. Johnson,

It gives me great pleasure to inform you that your proposal for the Crystal Fountain Culture and Vision Center of Reconciliation (CFCAVCOR), also known as the African American Cultural Center-Ethiopia Project, is approved by the Ethiopian Government. Please note that the Government of Ethiopia supports your proposal, and would like to encourage you to pursue your efforts in this endeavor.

Meanwhile let me bring you update on the recent changes in the Cabinet which are as follows:

Ministry of Finance and Economic Development	H.E. Ato Sufian Ahmed
Ministry of Culture and Tourism	H.E. Amb. Mohamed Drir
Ministry of Health	H.E. Dr. Tewodros Adhanom
Ministry of Justice	H.E. Ato Assefa Keseto

Should you need further assistance, please do not hesitate to contact me.

Sincerely,

Taye Atske Selassie
Consul General

3460 Wilshire Boulevard, Suite 308, Los Angeles, California 90010
Tel: (213) 365-6651, Fax: (213) 365-6670
www.ethioconsulate-la.org

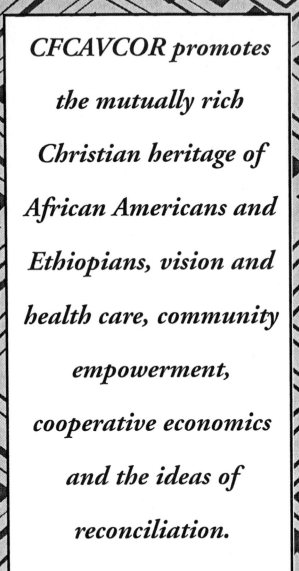

CFCAVCOR promotes the mutually rich Christian heritage of African Americans and Ethiopians, vision and health care, community empowerment, cooperative economics and the ideas of reconciliation.

THE CRYSTAL FOUNTAIN CULTURE AND VISION CENTER OF RECONCILIATION

P. O. Box 4434   Tele: 909.396.1201
Diamond Bar, CA 91765-0434   Fax: 909.860.7803
www.crystalfountain.org

Rev. Dr. Leonidas A. Johnson, President

EXECUTIVE SUMMARY
*The Crystal Fountain Culture and
Vision Center of Reconciliation*

The Crystal Fountain Culture and Vision Center of Reconciliation (CFCAVCOR) is a United States of America (USA) 501(c)(3) California nonprofit public benefit corporation founded by the Rev. Dr. Leonidas A. Johnson on April 15, 2004. CFCAVCOR is a product of Crystal Fountain Foundation. Crystal Fountain Foundation is a division of Crystal Fountain Ministries, Inc., a USA 501(c)(3) California nonprofit religious corporation founded by the Rev. Dr. Leonidas A. Johnson on September 26, 1997.

The mission of CFCAVCOR is *to promote the mutually rich Christian heritage of African Americans and Ethiopians, vision and health care, community empowerment, cooperative economics and the ideas of reconciliation.* A major activity of this organization consists of mobilizing African American aid to Africa and the promotion of the ideas of reconciliation. CFCAVCOR also promotes the development of business, trade, commerce, science, technology, industry and humanitarian aid through the idea of establishing an African American Cultural Center in Ethiopia.

CFCAVCOR, also known as **The African American Cultural Center—*ETHIOPIA!*** project, is organized into three major divisions: (1) The African American Center of Culture and Human Rights; (2) The Vocational Training and Vision Center(s); and, (3) The HIV Health Center(s). The CFCAVCOR Corporation is governed by a Board of Directors, who are appointed by the president, and consists of a nonvoting associate membership to help finance and support the goals of the organization. CFCAVCOR does not control property, finances or employ its associate members but may provide meetings, conventions, events, etc. for fellowship, networking, the exchange of culture, sport, art, science, industry and arrange incentives to enhance international trade, commerce and business opportunities for its members.

The national sponsor/partner of CFCAVCOR in Ethiopia is Justice for All/PF Fellowship, a duly recognized nongovernmental organization (NGO) previously known as Prison Fellowship Ethiopia (PFE). CFCAVCOR and Justice for All will jointly host various workshops/conferences in Ethiopia related to vision care, health/dental care, leadership training, human rights issues, HIV intervention, entrepreneur/business/commerce/trade/industry development, cultural exchange and appreciation, conflict resolution, and the ideas of reconciliation. We aim to use Justice for All/PF Fellowship staff, volunteers, affiliates and partners such as the Ethiopian Orthodox Tewahedo Church (EOTC) in accomplishing our goals in Ethiopia.

In His Service,
Rev. Dr. Leonidas A. Johnson
CFCAVCOR President

CFCAVCOR PILLARS OF FAITH

1. Christianity has historically had a positive impact in America and the African American community.

2. Christianity has historically had a positive impact in Ethiopia and the African Diaspora.

3. Vision is a physical, mental and spiritual process of discovery and is important to literacy, learning and spiritual awareness.

4. Medical/dental health care is important to human development and preservation; HIV/AIDS is a threat to world health.

5. Community empowerment can be fostered by using sports and the arts to bridge cultural gaps and by ensuring that human rights for all are protected.

6. Entrepreneurial development is a way to decrease poverty and increase business, trade, commerce, science, technology and industry.

7. The first step in reconciliation to God, self, and community involves humility.

Table of Illustrations

Ethiopia will quickly stretch out her hands to God. (Psalm 68:31, NKJV)

St. Mary of Zion Church Chapel (Aksum, Ethiopia) is said to contain the original Ark of the Covenant. Also believed to be the site of the original church erected by King Ezana in the 4th century after the adoption of Christianity, most likely this is the site of the very first church on African soil.

The Lion of Judah is the emblem of former Ethiopian Emperor Halie Sellassie (also known as Ras Tafari), who claimed to be a direct descendent of King Solomon and the Ethiopian Queen of Sheba. Location of image: anthropology museum, Institute of Ethiopian Studies, Addis Ababa University.

PHOTO ....**PAGE ix**

Ethiopian women carrying heavy loads, a daily chore.

PHOTO ....**PAGE xi**

The author giving an eye examination and instruction to a local Ethiopian health care provider. He volunteered as a Global Health Outreach medical team member in collaboration with Justice for All (Prison Fellowship Ethiopia), providing professional services to the Ethiopian Prison Authority. Photograph taken with permission by authorized personnel.

ILLUSTRATION... **PAGE xiii**

Major Affinity Blocs and the 10/40 Window. Patrick Johnstone, "Covering the Globe." In *Perspectives on the World Christian Movement: A Reader, Third Edition*, ed. Ralph D. Winter and Steven C. Hawthorne (Pasadena: William Carey Library, 1999), p. 545. Used by permission.

PHOTO ....**PAGE 1**

Ancient sacred Ethiopian manuscript from a remote Lake Tana island monastery, Bahar Dar.

GRAPH ....**PAGE 7**

Two Millennia of Evangelizing Peoples. Patrick Johnstone, "The Church is Bigger Than You Think." In *Perspectives* reader, p. 217. Used by permission.

ILLUSTRATION..**PAGE 27**

The Resistant Belt and the 10/40 Window. Patrick Johnstone, "Covering the Globe." In *Perspectives* reader, p. 542. Used by permission.

PHOTO ....**PAGE 55**

Bet Giyorgis Church, one of the most famous rock-hewn churches of Lalibela, Ethiopia and a United Nations Educational Scientific and Cultural Organization (UNESCO) world heritage site.

ILLUSTRATION...**PAGE 59**

Letter illustrating diplomatic communications and the author's due diligence to receive input and permission from the Ethiopian Government. When the letter was written, the African American Cultural Center—*ETHIOPIA!* (CFCAVCOR) was a project of the Crystal Fountain Foundation.

PHOTO ....**PAGE 61**

Lalibela ("Africa's Petra") is but one of Ethiopia's national treasures, ranking among the world's greatest historical sites. After large areas were marked off and trenches carved out, free-standing churches were chiseled out of solid rock. Pictured: Bet Amanuel Church.

GRAPH ....**PAGE 65**

World Evangelization and the 10/40 Window. Patrick Johnstone, "Covering the Globe." In *Perspectives* reader, p. 543. Used by permission.

PHOTO ....**PAGE 67**

One of many castles in the Royal Enclosure of Gonder. Gonder, a major attraction of Ethiopia's historical route, has been called Africa's Camelot.

ILLUSTRATION.......................................**PAGES 73, 75**

Sermon illustration designed by the author and executed by Cynthia Wierschen.

Photo .... Page 138

The author giving an eye examination and instruction to a local Ethiopian health care provider. He volunteered as a Global Health Outreach medical team member in collaboration with Justice for All (Prison Fellowship Ethiopia), providing professional services to the Ethiopian Prison Authority. Photograph taken with permission by authorized personnel.

Illustration... Page 139

Letter illustrating diplomatic communications and the author's due diligence to receive input and permission from the Ethiopian Government. When the letter was written, the African American Cultural Center—*ETHIOPIA!* (CFCAVCOR) had been established as an official 501(c)(3) nonprofit tax-exempt public benefit corporation.

Logo .... Page 141

A corporate symbol for CFCAVCOR designed by the author and executed by Gail Oliver.

Except as noted, all photographs are by the author.

CALL TO ACTION

The African American Cultural Center—*ETHIOPIA!* Operation Close the Window

† **Attention, African American Soldiers of the Cross!** †
God is raising up an army of African American missionaries!

The African American Church is beginning to awaken from its slumber. Do you feel God rousing you, mustering you for His army?

Don't delay, respond today! Answer God's missionary call to—and radiating from—Ethiopia, the kingdom of Sheba, legendary home of the Ark, our Jerusalem. Join an existing cadre for Operation Close the Window or start one in your church or organization.

YES! I want to take part in Operation Close the Window!

Rush me an enrollment packet for

☐ Individual ☐ Committee or Group

☐ Congregation ☐ Nonprofit
Organization

☐ Corporation/Business

Name: _____

Organization: _____

Address: _____

City/State/Zip: _____

Phone: _____

Email: _____

The Crystal Fountain Culture and Vision Center of Reconciliation (CFCAVCOR)
Rev. Dr. Leonidas A. Johnson
P. O. Box 4434 • Diamond Bar, CA 91765-0434, USA
Phone: (909) 396-1201 • Fax: (909) 860-7803

NOTES

_____

_____

_____

_____

_____

_____

_____

_____

_____

_____

_____

_____

_____

_____

_____

_____

Other Titles from William Carey Library

African-American Experience in World Mission: A Call Beyond Community
Vaughn J. Walston & Robert J. Stevens, eds.

Venture into the world of overseas missions from an African-American perspective. This collection of articles takes you deep into the history of missions in the African-American community. You will learn of the struggles to stay connected to the world of missions in spite of great obstacles, read of unique cultural experiences while traveling abroad, and feel God's heart for fulfilling the Great Commission both in the African-American community and beyond.

WCL609-9 · ISBN: 0878086099

Perspectives on the World Christian Movement, A Reader, 1999 Edition
Ralph Winter & Steve Hawthorne, eds.

Perspectives on the World Christian Movement (third edition) is a collection of readings exploring the biblical, historical, cultural, and strategic dimensions of world evangelization. Writings from more than 90 mission scholars and practitioners introduce lay people and students to the astounding potential of the global Christian movement.

WCL289-1 · ISBN: 0878082891

Printed in the United States
58949LVS00002B/73-165

9780878 083480